Mary Dwinell Chellis

At Lion's Mouth

Mary Dwinell Chellis

At Lion's Mouth

ISBN/EAN: 9783743341937

Manufactured in Europe, USA, Canada, Australia, Japa

Cover: Foto ©Andreas Hilbeck / pixelio.de

Manufactured and distributed by brebook publishing software (www.brebook.com)

Mary Dwinell Chellis

At Lion's Mouth

"TAKE A GLASS OF SOMETHING, TOM."—Page 100.

AT LION'S MOUTH.

BY

MISS MARY DWINELL CHELLIS,

AUTHOR OF 'TEMPERANCE DOCTOR,' 'OUT OF THE FIRE,' 'AUNT DINAH'S PLEDGE,' ETC.

——▶◆◀——

NEW YORK:
National Temperance Society and Publication House,
58 READE STREET.
1872.

Entered according to Act of Congress, in the year 1872, by

J. N. STEARNS,

In the Office of the Librarian of Congress, at Washington, D. C.

John Ross & Co., Printers, 27 Rose Street, New York.

CONTENTS.

CHAPTER I.
Darkening Clouds and Breaking Hearts, - - - 9

CHAPTER II.
One Gleaming Light, One Dauntless Will, - 53

CHAPTER III.
The Strongest and the Vilest must own God's Sovereign Power, - - - - - - - 103

CHAPTER IV.
Slowly but surely God's Purposes are Wrought, - 153

CHAPTER V.
The Darkest Way ofttimes shall Lead to Glorious Day, 205

CHAPTER VI.

The Tempter and the Tempted must Each his Burdens bear, - - - - - - - - 255

CHAPTER VII.

Alone with God, the Guilty Soul dares Offer no Excuse for Sin, - - - - - - - - 303

CHAPTER VIII.

Joys are but Sweeter for the Sorrows Past, 356

At Lion's Mouth.

CHAPTER I.

DARKENING CLOUDS AND BREAKING HEARTS.

IT was a dull, dreary day in Autumn. The leafless trees stood sharply outlined against a dark, lowering sky, athwart which drifted heavy masses of threatening clouds. No ray of sunlight enlivened the gloom. The poor felt their poverty more keenly; the sorrowing sorrowed more despairingly.

To one poor woman this day seemed to have gathered in itself all the misery and wretchedness of her life. Alone, since early morning, in a hut which afforded slight protection from the elements, she became so restless that longer waiting was impossible.

There was little of woman's ordinary work to occupy her time: no beautifying her home; no cooking, except as she prepared, in a rude way, the scanty food provided for a single meal. Occasionally her husband or son demanded her services to repair some old garment; but never a piece of sewing, the accomplishment of which would bring her nearer to some desired good. The fire was out, and there was nothing with which to replenish it. She drew around her shoulders a coarse woollen shawl, tied a faded cotton handkerchief over her abundant gray hair, and, taking a basket, went out to look for chips.

Jim Magee's hut was near a large river, on the banks of which, a mile distant, hummed and wrought the machinery of a score of mills. There was work for all who desired good, honest labor; abundance of food, and pleasant, cheerful homes. The woman looked towards the city, wishing vaguely that she might have some share in its prosperity. Then she walked on, stopping occasionally to brush aside a heap of leaves, or peer into some water-worn gully, snatching with eager hand the smallest twig or bit of wood.

A scrap of old newspaper fluttered before her. She was never much of a reader, and for years had seldom looked into a book; but now, for want of other objects of attention, she picked up the paper, seated herself at the foot of an old willow, and began to read. Perhaps I should say she attempted to spell out the words; for, in reality, she found it difficult to do even this. Fortunately, there was one story complete, so short and simple that she was able to comprehend it. A little girl had been the means of leading her parents to a better life; and so engrossed was the reader, that she did not notice the approach of a young man, until he called sharply, "Come home, mother. There's somebody there. Don't stop to ask questions, but come along."

The woman rose quickly, concealed the paper in the folds of her dress, and followed her son. At the door, he looked in, then waited for her to come up. "I've got into trouble," he said, in a low tone. "We had a bit of a row, and I threw a stone that hit a little girl, instead of a fellow I meant it should. She's hurt bad, but there ain't no bones broke. I asked Patsy to find out, and she's sure. I brought her home."

"What for, Tom?" asked his mother absently. "We hain't got nothing for ourselves. Where's her home?"

"Hain't got none. Worse off than we be. Father's jugged for ten years; and the woman she's lived with wouldn't have her. Said, if I didn't take her out the way, she'd call a p'leeceman."

"Will she die, Tom?"

"'Tain't likely. Such don't die easy. If she should, though—"

"You'd be the one that killed her," added his mother, completing the sentence. "How'd you get her here?"

"She walked part the way; then she kind of fainted, and I brought her the rest. I tell you, she'd be pretty if she was clean. Patsy said she'd come over and see about doctoring her up. I guess you'll get along together first-rate."

"But we hain't got no wood, nor no victuals. Then your father?"

"He's off down the river, for a month or two. Told me to tell you. Somebody's hired him. Shouldn't brought her if he was going to be round."

Within, upon a scantily covered straw bed, the injured child lay, staring vacantly at the smoke-blackened walls, and wondering if she would be allowed to remain in this poor place through the night. The stone thrown by Tom Magee had struck her right arm above the elbow, inflicting a severe bruise. Its force was nearly spent before reaching her, else the result would have been serious. As it was, she had fallen heavily upon the rough pavement, more from weakness and fright than any other cause.

Homeless and friendless, when a young man raised her in his arms, expressing sincere sorrow for the accident, the kind words were so welcome that she freely forgave him. This young man was not accustomed to hearing or speaking kind words.

He could remember when his mother would lay her hand upon his head, and call him her "dear boy." But that was long ago, before he had grown hard, and rough, and cruel; before the innocent look of childhood had gone from his face, and the tenderness from his heart.

Duke Moran had been arrested for robbery, tried, found guilty, and sentenced to ten years' hard labor in the State prison. He was a brutal, savage fellow, who had abused his wife until death came to her release, and ill-treated his little daughter, although she clung to him with the most devoted fondness. He had been away now six weeks, and the child crept about dreamily, receiving food from one and another, while she slept in a corner of a room formerly occupied by her father. Only that morning she had been told that she could not stay there another night, and all day she had been wishing she could go to her mother. It was little she knew of her Heavenly Father; but she needed help; and so, in her ignorant way, she asked God to help her. Doubt not her prayer was answered; for surely some new influence moved Tom Magee to pity. Ordinarily, he would have rushed away when danger threatened. He might have killed little Kate Moran; and this thought was uppermost in his mind when he sprang towards her. When told that no one would give her shelter, he asked if she would go home with him. "Yes," she answered, "I'll go anywhere." "Sure, why shouldn't she?" said an Irish woman standing near. "She's nobody belonging to her, now Duke's shut up."

"Take her out of the way, or we'll have you 'rested!" now exclaimed the woman who had promised Duke that she would look after his child. "Take her along with you, and don't bring her back."

By this time a crowd began to gather, and, Kate having somewhat recovered from her fall, Tom Magee asked her to follow him. She walked very slowly, yet still struggled on until they were beyond the city limits, when she fell, and, as he told his mother, he carried her the remainder of the way. He stopped for a little to talk with Patsy Quinn, an old woman who lived at what was called Lion's Mouth, where a branch of the river went eddying in and out among some venerable willows. Patsy was quite an oracle, in her way; and the young man was greatly relieved when told that Kate Moran would "come round all right."

As Mrs. Magee went in to make the acquaintance of the child so strangely brought to her home, a quivering voice murmured: "Don't send me away. I'm so tired, and so hungry, I can't go; and my arm hurts me, oh! so bad."

"No, dear, I won't send you away," was the reply. "You shall stay and get rested; and perhaps I'll keep you for my little girl."

"Will you give me something to eat? Please do, I'm so hungry."

"I'll fetch something," said Tom, darting from the house. He was almost at Lion's Mouth, when he met their neighbor, carrying a tin pail and a bundle of herbs. "Where now?" she asked. "Anything the matter?"

"I'm after something to eat. The child's hungry, and must eat."

"I know it," was the quick response,

"as bad off for being hungry as she is for being hurt. I've got something for her here in my pail; so you needn't go down the river, and like as not come back drunk."

"I ain't going down the river, Patsy Quinn. What made you think of that?"

"I can tell what lads like you think most of," said the old woman. "It's just the drink—curse it! and curse them that sells it!" she added, with bitter emphasis. Then she relapsed into silence, while her companion strode on before her. He had money in his pocket, which he would have spent for liquor but for the new responsibility he had assumed, and Patsy's caution was not ill-timed.

"Well, Mis Magee, you and I've got a job on hand, it seems," said the neighbor, laying her bundle of herbs on an old pine table. "I've brought some good medicine for little girls," she continued, going into the bedroom. "Here's some bread."

The proffered food was snatched eagerly without one murmured thank; and as soon as it was eaten, a thin hand was extended for more. A second slice seemed scarcely less welcome than the first.

"Now, stop awhile in the eating, and let's see what I can do for your arm," said Patsy cheerfully. "Does it ache?"

"Yes, ma'am. But the bread was so good I 'most forgot the ache. Can't I have another piece, to-day?"

"To-day!" repeated the woman, tears standing in her eyes. "To be sure you can. You can have some this minute. It's dreadful to be hungry; I know by experience. But now, thank God! I've enough. We must have some fire here. There's plenty of cut wood in Riley's yard. If you've got a quarter, Tom Magee, you'd better go down and buy some. Take it up in a hand-cart, and you will save something. Will you do it?"

"Yes. And hadn't I better get some flour?"

"Get some bread, and be quick about it. The wind blows through this old shell like it would through a sieve; and that child ought to be kept warm. You want her to get well."

"Perhaps I'll go to mother," murmured little Kate. "I asked God to let me, or else send somebody to take care of me. Don't you think he heard? Mother said he always hears us when we ask him."

"Likely he does, then," was the cold reply. "Any way, you'll be took care of; so you needn't worry."

"She said perhaps I might be *her* little girl," rejoined the child, looking to Mrs. Magee, who watched her anxiously. "He said he'd take care of me, too—that man that hurt me; he didn't mean to."

"I can't do much without a fire," remarked Patsy, taking a survey of the cheerless room. "We must have some hot water, and my herbs must be steeped. Get the stove ready for a fire 'gainst the wood comes, and get out the kittles."

Mrs. Magee, glad to be told what to do,

at once set about clearing the stove of ashes. Then she brought forward an old tin tea-kettle and an iron skillet, these two articles comprising the better part of her cooking utensils. Sooner than could have been expected, Tom returned with a hand-cart full of wood, a loaf of bread, and some crackers.

"It didn't take much money, Tom?"

"Not much," he answered, smiling grimly; "not half I thought 'twould. I promised to go back with the cart."

"Got any money left?" He displayed a handful of pennies. "Then get some tea for your mother, and see how it will seem to make her comfortable. What with you and your father, she has an awful life. You see, I know how 'tis. She'd rather die than live."

"I'll get some tea," replied Tom; "you may depend on that. Guess I've had liquor enough for one day. Any way, I'll make it do."

A good fire soon burned in the rusty

stove, and little Kate Moran enjoyed the luxury of a warm bath; after which she was wrapped in a garment entitled to the one merit of being clean. Others might have laughed at her grotesque appearance; but she was satisfied. Some hot herbs were bound upon her arm, and then she was left to sleep.

"Now, just eat a little yourself, Mis Magee," urged Patsy Quinn. "I know you're hungry, or you would be if you wa'n't so discouraged."

"What's to hinder my being discouraged!" was the reply. "Things grow worse and worse. Tom says his father's gone. And that girl—I don't see what made Tom fetch her here. Not but what I'd like to have her, if we had anything to live on. She makes me think of little Mary. I thought 'twould kill me when she died; but now I'm glad she's out of the way."

"Don't talk that way, Mis Magee. I can't bear it. I try not to remember

what's happened to me. I just want to
think I've always been old Patsy Quinn,
not a year younger than I am now. Mis
Magee, do you mind that you was a young
thing once, like that one in there?"

"Yes, and 'most as bad off. Father was
a drunkard; so I didn't have much but
hard times when I was a girl. I worked,
and he took 'most all my wages. Since
I've been married to Jim, things hain't been
much better. When Tom was a baby, I
used to be happier than I ever was before;
but he's no good to me now. If I wa'n't
afraid of what's beyond, I'd throw myself
into the river."

"Don't do that, Mis Magee; it's a long
road that has no turn—just remember that!
And then, this has been a dreadful discouraging day. I've been 'most discouraged myself; though I hadn't ought to be—I'm
sure of a living as long as I can work.
I've more washing than I know how to do;
and they're always wanting me in the mill."

"Yes," answered her companion. "But you see it ain't no use for me to work. Jim would take every cent I earned."

"He's gone, now."

"Yes, but he'll be back. He would if I got things a little more comfortable; I've tried it. He won't have that child here no way, when he comes. You ought to know better than to fetch her."

"Tom couldn't help it very well," answered Patsy. "He's been in a good many fights, and made a good many enemies. There's enough that would be glad to see him in trouble. 'Twouldn't took much to finish that child when he found her. She's been abused and half starved. I've heard her mother was a good woman; but Duke's the very devil when he's been drinking. He won't get half he deserves in ten years. It's a good thing for his child that he's out of the way; though folks say, sometimes he made everything of her."

So the two women talked on, while the

child slept. "Tom's coming," at length said the visitor. "You'd better try and make things a little comfortable. Perhaps he won't go off again to-night if you do. It's going to be a lonesome night. I'm expecting rain."

Tom came in, and, taking two small packages from his pocket, threw them into his mother's lap, saying, "There's some tea and some sugar. You can have a cup of tea, and I guess I should like some, too. You needn't be afraid to use all you want. I'm going to work to-morrow, and I'll get some more. Hain't got a cent left. How's Kate?"

"Fast asleep," was the answer to this question. "Tell you what, Tom, I've a notion of taking that little girl to live with me. I can do better by her than you will, and she needs a good deal done for her."

"It'll take two to make that bargain, and perhaps three," was the reply.

"Why? What's come over you, Tom?

She's got to have something to eat, and 'tain't much your mother has to spare, these days. I'd bring her round well quicker than you will."

"See here, Patsy," exclaimed the young man, "what are you driving at? I'm able to earn enough for us all. I fetched her home, and she'll stay here."

"To be sure, Tom. Everybody says you can work like a tiger; but the drink's the trouble. When it gets down your throat, there's the devil to pay, and nothing for baker or butcher. That's how 'tis."

Mrs. Magee, who was engaged in preparing supper, watched the two furtively, expecting to hear angry words from her son, and wishing that her neighbor would talk differently. Patsy, however, felt no misgivings. She had once rendered Tom Magee a signal service, and was therefore privileged.

"Set down, and drink some tea with us," at length said the poor woman.

"Yes, set down," urged Tom, "there's enough for all. Give Kate some, too, and a cracker."

But the child was asleep; and just then sleep was better for her than tea or crackers. An hour later, as the darkness of night was closing round them, mother and son were left alone.

"We don't often have such a fire," remarked Mrs. Magee, extending her hands to catch the genial warmth.

"No," was the answer given. "We ought to, though. It's bad enough here with a fire. The cracks grow wider, and to-night the wind blows like mad. Father went 'cause things are so bad."

"They might be better. He's the one to blame," said his wife. "I'd work if 'twould do any good. We'll be flooded 'fore morning," she added, as the first drops of rain beat against the windows. "Patsy's got home by this time. I'm glad of that. She's a good neighbor. I don't know what we'd done without her; and I don't know what we'll do any way. Your father might come back any time, and then—"

"There'd be a row," carelessly added the son. "There ain't no love lost between us, any time; and to-day he tried to bully me out of what money I had. He didn't get it, though, and it's lucky all round he didn't."

"Do you believe he'll stay away?"

"Yes," answered Tom with an oath. "There ain't nothing for him here, and he'll try a new place till he gets sick of that. We'd move out of this old place, if 'twa'n't for fishing; and, besides, there's more elbow room. There's some good, being this side."

"What you going to do to-morrow?" asked Mrs. Magee.

"Work for Riley. He's got a hard job on hand, and promised good pay." As the young man talked, he stopped now and then to listen for a sound from the bedroom. "She won't die, mother?" he said.

"She don't look like it," was the reply.

It was dull business for Tom Magee, sitting there with only his mother for company, and a vague dread of evil overshadowing him. "I wish I had something to read," he exclaimed impatiently. "There ain't so much as a scrap of newspaper in the house."

"Yes, there is," responded his mother, "just a scrap. I found it out-doors to-day, but I couldn't read it very well. Wish you'd read it to me."

"Let's have it, then," said Tom ungraciously. "I guess it's a goodish story," he remarked, after he had lighted a candle and glanced at the paper. "'Tain't my sort, but I'll read it to you. Want to keep it?" he asked, after the reading was ended. "That little girl was some like Kate. Let's have some more fire. It's the blackest night we've had, this fall. We'll be afloat if it keeps on at this rate."

The evening seemed long to these people, who knew the lapse of time only by the ringing of the city bells. At nine o'clock, Tom went up some half-broken stairs into a small, unfinished garret, where he threw himself upon a bed, and endeavored to sleep. More entirely free from the influence of liquor than he had been at night for many months, he could not but reflect upon the strange events of the day. Then the story which he had just read, so unlike his usual reading. This was intended to teach some religious truth, and he knew absolutely nothing of religion. Except that in school he had read a few verses from the Bible, as a part of regular school exercise, he did not remember of ever opening the Holy Book. The Sabbath was to him as other days, while he profaned the name of God without thought of his sin. "You'll end your life in State's prison or on the gallows," had been said to him more than once; and there certainly seemed good reason for the prediction. He laughed derisively; yet he had been suspected of many petty thefts, and he knew that no one would trust him. These were not pleasant reflections in his present mood.

Mrs. Magee lay down beside the sleeping child, and, weary as she was, was soon oblivious of all which had transpired. Her son was moving about the kitchen when she awoke, and the early bells had already rung out their call.

Tom's first enquiry was for the child. "You'll take good care of her, won't you, mother?" he said. "It's been pouring rain every minute since I went up-stairs last night, and 'twouldn't be strange if Riley's yard's under water. There's water enough on the floor to wash it, and 'twouldn't hurt us to be a little cleaner. Guess you've got enough to eat to-day, and I'll be back by dark."

It was early for Tom Magee to be out, but Patsy Quinn was watching for him, and, to escape the rain, he went into her house while he answered her questions.

"Drink some coffee," she said, pouring a generous quantity into a bowl. "I can't afford sugar and milk, but it's hot, and 'twill do you good—more good than the stuff that generally goes down your throat. Why don't you swear off, and see what you can do? You might be somebody."

"Ain't I somebody now?"

"You're old Jim Magee's boy, getting to be worse than the old man, and going straight to the devil!"

"You've made a mistake. I'm going to Riley's wood-yard," responded Tom, with an attempt to be facetious.

"The devil keeps open shop just beyond," retorted Patsy. "You'll be there within an hour."

"Sure of it, are you? I can keep out if I'm a mind to."

"Perhaps you could, and perhaps you couldn't. Folks say that, when anybody gets started drinking as you have, they have to keep on, whether they want to or not."

"That's a lie!" exclaimed Tom, emphasizing his assertion with an oath. "Needn't anybody tell this child he can't stop drinking liquor just any time."

"Then stop for to-day, and see how you make out."

"I will!" Another oath sealed the promise. "I'll be round about dark, and let you see what I've earned; going to carry it all home to the old woman and the baby."

Laughing coarsely, as he said this, he went out into the storm; and his friend had forgotten to ask for little Kate Moran.

"Never mind," she soliloquized, "I've give him some hits, and may be 'twas in the right way. If he don't drink to-day, all the better for Mis Magee. I'll try and find time to run up there."

A bowl of coffee, a slice of bread, and some cold meat furnished a sumptuous breakfast for the poor woman, and then she commenced her daily task. Allowing herself no rest at noon, she gained time for a call to her neighbor up the river. It had ceased raining, though the wind still continued to blow; yet she heeded neither the heavy mud nor the pools of water that lay in her path—she was intent only upon reaching her destination.

A child's face was pressed to the window as she came in sight, and the door was opened for her before she could lift the latch.

"Up and dressed!" she exclaimed, speaking to little Kate Moran. "I didn't expect to see you dressed for a week. How do you feel, to-day?"

"Better, ma'am."

"I'm afraid she ain't much better," said Mrs. Magee; "but she got tired staying in the bedroom, so I fixed her up by the window, where she could look out, though I don't know what she'd see. She won't take cold, will she?"

"Guess there's no danger; but it's always best to be careful. Does your arm ache?" she asked, turning to the child.

"Yes, ma'am, some; but I'm warm, and I ain't hungry. She gave me bread and crackers, all I wanted."

"And did you have some for yourself, Mis Magee?"

"All I wanted," was the reply. "I hain't been much hungry to-day. I've kept round to work most the time."

"I should know you had. Things look more comfortable than they did yesterday; and you've washed all Kate's clothes. Now, if you'd paste some paper over the cracks, 'twouldn't take so much wood to keep you warm. That's what I do, and save wood. I've been thinking about you all day, and hurried so I could get time to come up. I guess that little girl better go to bed, or else set up here by the stove."

"She read to me," said Mrs. Magee, after the child was comfortably seated near the stove. "She reads 'most as well as Tom, and I like to hear her."

"What did she read?"

"My story. I picked it up out-doors, yesterday."

Then Patsy must needs hear, and again Kate read the simple story, so fraught with instruction. "Strange how you come to be such a scholar!" This was the comment made; but it was not this which brought tears to the eyes of the listener. "Ever been to school?"

"Not many days," was the reply. "Mother told me the letters before she died, and I've got some books like this paper would be folded up. A lady gave them to me, but I can't make out all the words."

There was some further conversation, after which the little reader confessed herself tired, and gladly lay down to sleep.

"How's gone the day?" then asked Patsy Quinn.

"I don't know," was the answer of her companion; "I can't quite make out. Things seem strange, and I'm afraid what'll happen when Tom comes. He's 'most as bad as Jim when he's been drinking; and there mustn't no harm come to Kate Moran while she's here. I wish you'd take her."

"I would, Mis Magee; but, you see, Tom won't give her up as he feels now. I'll be ready, though, to step in if anything happens. You'd miss her."

"Yes; but I'd rather she'd go 'fore I git my heart set on her. She's just like a baby, she's so good. Like the story. I can't say it, Patsy, but may be you know what I mean. I'm all stirred up in my feelings, and seems as though I was waiting for something to happen."

Her friend made no reply to this. These poor women, wholly unaccustomed to the analysis of their feelings, lacked words to describe the new emotions which moved them. They could, however, sympathize with each other, and the silence was not irksome.

"If I can't do anything for you, I guess I'd better go," at length said the visitor,

"I want to be home 'fore dark. And mind, Mis Magee, when Tom comes, don't talk discouraging. Praise him if he brings anything; and don't find fault if he don't. Boys like to be praised; and he's only a lad, for all his size. You mind what I say."

"Yes; but likely I won't see Tom tonight."

Not see Tom! Indeed she would. He was at the door of Patsy Quinn's house when she came in sight, and directly she shouted, "Good for you, my lad. What's in your cart?"

"Wood, and things to eat. I've worked like two niggers, and got all I've earned with me."

"Good again, my lad; come in, and I'll give you more coffee. Had you anything to drink since morning?"

"Cold water, and not a drop of anything stronger. I told you, and I've kept my word. Been up to the old house?"

"Yes; all's right. That girl won't die yet

awhile. If your father comes home, bring her to me, will you?"

"I'd have to," was the reply. "The old man's ugly, and she ain't going to be abused by him or anybody else."

"That's right, Tom. Won't you have the coffee?"

"No; I'll push along home." And, suiting the action to the word, the young man moved on.

"Hain't drinked a drop," said Patsy Quinn, half aloud. "'Twa'n't no use to coax him, I knew that, and didn't expect the other way'd work. But he hain't drinked a drop. I mind when my boy—" Here the speaker drew one hand across her forehead, looked vacantly up and down the river, and then entered her lonely dwelling.

At the same time, Mrs. Magee was watching, anxiously waiting, as she had said, for something to happen. A slight sound from the bedroom called her attention, and scarcely had she returned to the window when

Tom appeared. "I'm glad you've come," she said, as he entered.

"How is she?" he asked, as though there was but one person in the world to whom this pronoun could be applied. "She ain't going to die?"

"Not this time. She's better, all but her arm; and she ain't hungry nor cold. Please, man, won't you come here?"

Tom waited for no second summons. He was gazing down into the sweet, pale face of Kate Moran, when she said, "I'm ever so much better, and you was ever so good to bring me here. Your mother's took care of me all day, and my arm don't hurt much now. Ain't you a good man?"

"Guess not," was the answer to this question. "If I'd been good, I shouldn't hurt you."

"But you was sorry for that. Mother said, when we was sorry, God forgives us. You tell God, and he'll forgive you."

"A sermon, and the very queerest preacher," thought Tom. "Wouldn't the boys laugh if they heard her!"

"You'll let me stay here, won't you? I'll work real hard if you'll let me, and I won't eat but little. I won't cost much."

Such pleading! For a moment the heart of the young man was tender as a woman's; while, in tones modulated to strange gentleness, he assured the child that he would care for her.

"You're so good," she murmured, in her simplicity; while he knew that he was a vile, wicked wretch.

"Never done no good in all my life. Ain't fit to look at her. No, I ain't. Old Jim Magee's boy; dirty, ragged, and saucy. Guess if God ever made such a boy, he's forgot it before now. Wonder how 'twould seem to live like other folks!"

At this point in his soliloquy, a low, musical whistle escaped his lips, and Kate asked, "Was that you whistled?"

"I suppose 'twas," he replied. "I didn't mean to."

"Didn't? It sounded 'most like a bird. I had a bird once, in a cage, before mother died. He could whistle."

Again the weary eyes closed, and Tom went into the kitchen, where his mother was doing her best to prepare a comfortable supper from very scanty materials.

"Hold on!" he exclaimed, "we'll have something better than what you've got there. I've got some meat and a peck of potatoes. We'll have a bully supper. I'm hungry's a bear, but I'll wait for the meat. There's enough for breakfast, too; and, to-morrow, I'll bring some more. I'm going to work. If the old man won't show himself for six months, we might live like other folks."

"Why, Tom, my boy!" The poor woman could say no more, as she examined the several parcels which were placed before her. "Where'd you get so much?"

"Bought it, and paid for it all, to-day. Been to work every minute."

Just then was heard a prolonged hoot,

which simple people would have accredited to the ill-omened bird of night, but which Tom Magee recognized as the signal-call of his boon companions. In his vague aspirations for a better life, he had quite forgotten "The Owls," of which he was a prominent member. He had been missed from his accustomed haunts, and must give an account of himself; perhaps, also, he was expected to join a drunken orgy, or assist in the perpetration of some crime. The hoot was repeated.

"That ain't no owl," said his mother.

"Guess not," was the reply; "it's some of them fools over the river. Wish they'd mind their business. I want my supper."

"Ain't you going to eat it?"

"Yes; so go ahead with your cooking. I'll have to go, but I'll come back if I'm alive." And, muttering a succession of oaths, he left the house.

"Who's here?" he asked, in a surly tone.

"I myself," answered a familiar voice.

"What you want?"

"Want you. The boys are on the other side. There's fun ahead, and we want you to take your share. If owls keep close all day, they come out at night. You're an Owl."

Of course, this communication was interlarded with oaths, but its profanity was tolerable compared with that of the response. The two continued to talk in much the same strain; and, at length, a coarse joke was ventured in regard to Kate Moran. Then Tom's anger was fully aroused, and as a matter of safety the offender retreated.

"You refuse to meet 'The Owls'?"

"I *do* refuse to meet 'The Owls,'" answered Tom, with a fearful imprecation. "They can do what they're a mind to about it. I'll fight the whole bilin of 'em any time when they're ready. Now be off with you, or I'll pitch you into the water, neck and heels."

The dipping of oars assured the speaker

that his last argument had not been without effect.

"Settled for once," was the comment. "There'll be a row, but they won't be back to-night. I've put a flea in one Owl's ear. Patsy heard the hoot, and she'll be on the lookout. Wonder where her boy is? Wonder, too, what's come to this boy? Didn't Kate hit wide when she talked about my being good? Wonder what I brought her home for? Fool for doing it, and get myself into a scrape. What's come over me? Can't be I'm the Big Owl? Wish somebody'd tell me what's the matter; Patsy might do it. She's smart, and if she does know all about me, 'tain't no matter. She's a good one to keep a secret. If she hadn't, I'd seen trouble."

Mrs. Magee opened the door to look out, and this reminded her son of the supper she was preparing. Acting upon the advice she had received, she spread her table as neatly as possible, and made the best display of the scanty furniture.

"Seems to me things look better'n common, mother. Guess you've been slickin' up."

"Yes," was the mother's reply to this welcome appreciation of her efforts. "I've been to work. Patsy says we ought to paste paper over the cracks and make it warmer."

"Guess she's right. She most always is. She's going to take *her* when the old man comes. If I ain't here, tell her to run straight for Lion's Mouth. If it's in the night, put her out the bedroom window, and I'll take her. Wish he was in the bottom of the river."

"Don't, Tom, that's wicked. Wish he'd do better."

"'Tain't no use. There ain't a worse sot than Jim Magee. Guess he's one of the sort that can't stop or *won't* stop."

Tom was talking strangely for one like him; and his mother, not knowing how to reply, was silent. The thought of her husband brought back the gloom and despondency which usually oppressed her. She feared his return, and in her heart echoed the wish she had condemned as wicked. Yet she did not give expression to her fears. Supper was placed on the table, and eaten with evident relish.

"Now, I'd go down and see Patsy if 'twan't for leaving you alone," said the young man; and, observing a look of incredulity upon his mother's face, he added, "I wouldn't go anywhere else. That Owl went over the river with his wings spread. He won't be back to-night. Want I should stay with you?"

"Yes, Tom; I'm dreadful lonesome. I'm afraid, too. Seems as though something'd happen."

The seeming proved a reality. These words were hardly spoken when the door opened, and Jim Magee entered. "Glad you've got some supper," was his gruff salutation. "Start round, old woman, and bring on the best you've got. Thought I'd come home and make a visit. Hit on a good time. Fine doings, when I'm gone. Let's have some meat; and the quicker the better." Having thus insulted his wife, he addressed his son, in a tone no less offensive. "I'll take that money, now, and teach you better manners when I've had my supper."

"No, you won't," was the reply. "I've had enough of your manners. Best thing you can do is to mind your own business. I'm able to take care of myself."

"We'll see about that."

"Yes, we'll see."

Glances were exchanged between mother and son, the latter placing his chair against the bedroom door. There was no alternative but to bring forward the stores intended for another day. Refusal would only exasperate the hungry man. When he was seated at the table, eating ravenously, Tom left the house. Mrs. Magee understood what was expected of her, and presently little Kate Moran was placed in the arms of her son.

"Don't be afraid," he whispered, "I'll take care of you." And, wrapping a shawl closely about her, he hastened to a place of safety. "Here, Patsy," he exclaimed, when this was reached. "We've got company at our house. The old man's come, and I must go straight back. I'll bring her clothes. Tell her, so she'll know. 'Twon't do for me to stop."

"That owl hooted for you, Tom."

"S'pose it did; but 'twon't hoot again, this side, to-night."

He was gone; and there sat the child, glancing around, as though seeking acquaintance with her new surroundings.

"Be you cold?" asked her companion.

"No, ma'am. I ain't hungry, neither. But what made that man bring me away from his house?" This question was answered frankly to Kate's comprehension. "I know," she said, with a sigh. "I've seen folks so."

It was well that Tom Magee returned quickly, else he might have been motherless, and his father a murderer. A violent altercation ensued; but his defiant manner won the victory.

A long night was that which followed. Newly formed resolves were nearly abandoned, as one disheartening thought after another presented itself. What good in trying to do well? Why not go on, and let the worst come, if it would? Up to this time, the young man had never thought of abandoning entirely the use of intoxicating liquor. It was only to drink less; to work more, dress better, and live like other people. He was sixteen years of age; in point of law, subject to his father, who could claim his wages. No use to work, and have it all go down the old man's throat. Winter was at hand, and his mother for some reason—he thought tenderly of his mother—must be provided with many comforts. Kate Moran, too. The woman who had received her must not be left to furnish her support.

In his unrest, he would have drunk to bring forgetfulness; but, fortunately, there was not a drop of liquid poison in the house. His throat was parched with thirst, and he awoke to a consciousness of the chains which bound him.

He heard the distant bells, and sprang from his bed while the stars were yet shining. There were lights here and there in the city, and he stood gazing at them, when his mother came out of the house, and stood beside him.

"Be you going?" she asked in a subdued tone.

"Yes," was the reply, "I'm going to work, and I'll get my breakfast at Patsy's. 'Twon't be best for me to see the old man."

"What'll *I* do?"

"I don't know, mother. Wish I did. If you hain't got enough to eat, go to Patsy's. I'll settle with her. If he was dead and out of the way, there'd be some chance for us. I don't see what folks like him live for."

"He wa'n't so bad as you when he wa'n't no older."

"Mother!"

"That's true, Tom. I remember. And he wa'n't so bad when we was first married. It's all the drink; and I'm afraid for you."

"May be you've reason. But don't worry. The old man'll go off after he's had some breakfast; and if you get lonesome, go down the river. Give me Kate's things, and I'll take them along. You'll see me at dark."

Tom Magee breakfasted at Lion's Mouth, where he ate and talked, at the same time receiving encouragement, while expressing many of his hopes and wishes. When it was light, he went to the wood-yard, worked steadily through the morning, at noon ate a lunch which he bought at the baker's, and resumed labor. In the afternoon, he delivered some wood at the house of a lady, who asked his assistance in removing a heavy piece of furniture; and here he saw a young man, not much older than himself, reclining upon a couch.

"I almost envy you your strength," remarked the occupant of the couch. "It is something for which you ought to thank God. To save my life, I could not do what you have just done."

"Perhaps you've been sick, and lost your strength," was the embarrassed reply.

"I have always been sick; or, at least, I never have been strong. I never expect to be strong in this world. And it seems hard, sometimes, because there is so much I want to do. I wish I could find some one to do my work for me."

"What you want done, sir?" asked Tom Magee respectfully. "Perhaps I might help you."

"I wish you could; but the work I want done isn't what you are accustomed to do."

"I might learn, sir. I'm called quick to learn."

"You've learned some things too quick, my friend."

"You're right, there. Guess I have." And involuntarily an oath escaped the speaker's lips.

"That's one wrong thing you've learned," was said quickly. "Don't you know it is a sin to swear?"

"Yes, sir, I've heard so; but I forgot."

"Don't forget again. Tell me your name, if you please, so I can write it in my list. I have a list of the names of some of my friends, and I should like to add yours."

"'Tain't a good name," said the young man, looking with wonder and admiration upon one who addressed him as friend. "Such as 'tis, you're welcome to it, though. I'm Tom Magee."

"You live up beyond Lion's Mouth."

"Yes, sir."

"Then I'm very glad to see you. I

have some little books here that I keep to give my friends, and I will give you one if you will read it. It is a story, and all the better perhaps for that. Will you read it?"

"Yes, sir."

"And will you come to see me sometimes, when you are at leisure, so that we can have a long talk about the work I want done?"

"Yes, sir, I'll come any time you say."

"Then come to-morrow evening."

Mrs. Richards manifested no impatience while her son conversed with this stranger; and, when he reached the door, she said pleasantly, "I hope we shall see you again. Wilbur will be disappointed if you break your engagement."

An awkward bow replied to this, and the door was closed.

"There's a large field for cultivation," remarked the invalid, adjusting the pillows of his couch.

"And have you faith in your ability to reclaim it?" asked the mother.

"If I plant, and you water, God may give the increase," was the response. "The Magees, father and son, are notorious for their wickedness; but they are not past hope. This Tom has good abilities, and, if I'm not mistaken, there's a generous heart hidden under a vast deal of rubbish."

"You are very hopeful, my son."

"My mother's own child. Who but you taught me to be hopeful and patient? If I had that fellow's strength, the world should be better for my living in it; and now I'm not satisfied to be wholly idle. If I can win Tom Magee to work for me, I may be doing good in two ways. If he reads the book I gave him, I shall be encouraged. Of course I shall pray for him, and you'll remember him, mother?"

Mrs. Richards smiled an assent, and, although having little expectation that the young man who had just left her house would redeem his promise, she did not express her distrust. If he should come, there would be an opportunity for some effort in his behalf; if he should not come, the words which had been spoken might not be entirely without effect.

CHAPTER II.

ONE GLEAMING LIGHT, ONE DAUNTLESS WILL.

"GONE too long, this time," said Mr. Riley, as his assistant drove into the yard. "Yes, sir; but the lady wanted some help in the house. I'll make it up." Not even a frown accompanied this reply, and the wood merchant looked the surprise which he felt. When did Tom Magee ever speak in that tone to one who reproved him?

"All right, Tom; nothing to make up," was said heartily. "We only want to get through with the orders."

The day's work was completed at dark, and the day's wages paid. Every cent was spent for food, and the young man was walking home, when his mother met him before he reached Lion's Mouth. Frightfully pale as she was, with dark circles around her eyes, and marks of violence upon her face, she did not need to say that she had suffered from a drunkard's fury. "O Tom! I've wanted you," she exclaimed, after a moment's scrutiny of her son. "I thought he'd kill me."

An oath was smothered, but the fire burned within as he asked, "Where is the old man?"

"I left him up there. I ran away, and I can't go back to-night. Patsy'll keep me, and you too. You'd better not go up."

How warm and pleasant was the little house whose doors were opened to receive them, and how cheerful was the voice which welcomed them! "Come in, friends. We'll make quite a family, to-night. Supper's waiting, and my little girl's getting sleepy."

"I don't know about stopping," replied Tom. "Guess I'd better keep on." Entreaty, however, prevailed, and he threw down his packages sullenly. Was not everything against him? No, not everything. Here were his mother and Kate trusting him, the latter waiting for a word of recognition. "Good-evening, sis," he said, going towards her.

"Good-evening. I'm glad you've come," she made answer.

"Be you? That's good. How do you do?"

"'Most well, only my arm," she replied truthfully. "That's going to get well. Ain't it nice here?"

"Very; you like it?"

"Yes, sir, only I'm afraid I hadn't ought to stay. I cost so much, and I can't work."

"But I can. You just get well, and I'll take care of the cost.—I didn't calculate on your taking the whole family," added Tom, turning to their hostess. "There's something for supper in them bundles, and I sha'n't carry them any further."

This addition to her supplies did not come amiss to Patsy Quinn, and soon the table was more generously spread; while she, affecting a cheerfulness she was far from feeling, urged her guests to partake of the food before them. When Tom put on his cap, she tied a hood upon her head, threw a large blanket-shawl over her shoulders, and said, "I'm going out a little while. Mis Magee, you and Kate can keep house; and, if anybody comes, tell them I shall be back before long. I sha'n't go a great ways."

It was not to walk, but to talk that she came out, as Tom well knew. She wished to consult with him in regard to his mother, and decide upon some course of action. When they were near the hut, she paused while her companion went forward. Soon she heard angry talking, and then a heavy fall.

"I've settled the old man for to-night," exclaimed Tom, coming out to her. "He struck me, and I levelled him. I've done enough for once. We'll go back, now."

"Not till you know how bad he's hurt," was the reply. "Go in and see."

"Not this child."

"Then I'll go in alone. There ain't no stir in the house, and may be he needs help."

"Then let him help himself," replied the son, and yet he followed his friend as she threw open the door of the hut.

Jim Magee was lying motionless, stunned by his fall; nevertheless, an application of water soon restored him, and, refusing all assistance, he rose to his feet, confronting the two who regarded him so differently. There was such hate in the son's heart that he could feel no pity. Yet he was treading the same path his father had trodden; degrading himself by the same habits, and fast going down to the same depths of infamy. "Like father, like son." For the first time he realized the full import of these words.

A tiger at bay never glared more ferociously at an escaped victim than did the drunkard at his son; but having tested their comparative strength, he did not care to renew the contest. His rage found expression in hideous oaths, and, when tired of this weapon of defence, he asked fiercely for his wife, demanding that she return home.

"I'll stand between you and mother in future," said Tom decidedly. "You won't abuse her much more when I'm round."

"Much good she'll get from you," was the sneering reply. "Go up-stairs, and mind your own business, while I look after the old woman."

"Come," now whispered Patsy, and without another word they left the house.

The time had seemed long to Mrs. Magee, suffering as she was with the fear of some new calamity; but now, reassured and comforted, she was glad to seek forgetfulness in sleep. Tom slept upon the floor that night, ready for any emergency; and before any one else was astir he visited his old home. When he returned, Patsy praised his energy, remarking, "You'll be somebody yet."

"I don't know about that," was the reply. "I'm 'most discouraged. I don't know but I'd try, if 'twould do any good. I could give up liquor. I know that, because I ain't drinked none this two days. But what's the use? The old man'll do his worst to keep me back; and the boys — I don't care for them, though. They'll be glad to keep out of my way after they find out I'm in earnest. Two came round yesterday, but Riley ordered them off, and I didn't help them about staying."

"Good for you, my lad. I've some hope of you. I'll help you all I can. Just count on that; and my help's worth something, if I ain't only a poor, lone woman."

"You're a brick, Patsy!" exclaimed the young man. And this compliment was received in the same spirit it was given. "Something strange happened to me yesterday, and I want to tell you about it," he added, after a short silence. And his companion signifying that she wished to hear, he proceeded to describe his interview with Wilbur Richards. "Now, I'm going just as I promised, but I'll be ashamed of myself forty times. I hain't got nothing fit to wear, and I ain't fit to talk with such as they be; but I'm going. I can learn to do 'most any kind of work, and I'm bound to help that fellow what he wants. He called me his friend, and there's the book he give me. I meant to read it last night, but I forgot it. You can read it, Patsy."

"I ain't much of a reader, but Katy'll read it to me," answered the woman. "You just go to Mis Richards, to-night, if you have to go on your knees; and you do just as that young man tells you. Why, folks say he's better than any of the ministers round here. He's a great scholar, too, for all he's such a strengthless thing. His mother's a lady, and he's all she's got."

"They've got money," said Tom Magee. "I wish I'd got as much as they have."

"You've got something better'n money, my lad. You've got health and strength. Would you change places with Wilbur Richards? Would you sell your strength for money?"

"No, that I wouldn't!" And the speaker drew himself up proudly as he uttered this emphatic negative. He had often boasted of his size and strength; and this boasting was not without reason. Something of this his companion was thinking as she said:

"If you was dressed up, you needn't be ashamed of your looks nowhere."

"No use to talk that," was the response. "I've got to wear these old clothes till I earn some better, and I don't know when that'll be. I want to make a bargain with you about mother and Kate. Mother ain't going up the river till the old man can behave himself decent, and that ain't likely to be very soon."

"We'll see about that. Your mother can cook your board and hers on my stove, and I sha'n't ask nothing for room if you'll let drink alone."

"There ain't no danger of my drinking, to-day," said Tom. "I wouldn't drink for nobody. Riley wants me to keep right on to work for him; but I sha'n't make no bargain till I've talked with that young fellow I see yesterday."

This assurance being given, the speaker examined his book while breakfast was being prepared; and the story, pleasantly told, so fixed his attention that he laid it aside with reluctance. It was very different from his usual reading, and, perhaps, for that reason impressed him more strongly. Before going to work he commended his mother to the care of their mutual friend, arranging that he should be notified if his father proved troublesome. Often during the day he looked towards Lion's Mouth, expecting to see a flag of distress; but, happily, none appeared.

"The Owls," however, gave token of their dissatisfaction and distress. Watching for their recreant brother, when he was engaged at a distance from the wood-yard they assailed him with questions couched in language befitting their pursuits. Tom Magee was in no mood to brook interference, as they would have known had they been sober; but, excited by liquor and the coolness of their reception, they ventured upon dangerous ground. There was danger of a fight, but, controlling himself with great effort, Tom defined his present position.

"Look here!" he exclaimed, "you've said enough; and, now, you'd better go about your business. I ain't a coward. You know that. I could knock your teeth down your throat, but I won't. I'll see you a week from to-night, and tell you what I've a mind to; but 'tain't no use hooting for me. Now, get out of my way."

At this the half-drunken rowdies were glad to retreat, and their old associate was left to his work. Impatient for the evening, and wishing time to make what preparations were possible, he completed his allotted task at an early hour.

"What's come over you, these three days?" asked his employer, after expressing entire satisfaction with his services. "You don't act like yourself. Folks tell me 'tain't safe to have you 'round. How's that? Tell the truth square out, so I can know what to depend on. I want a good, trusty hand for the winter, and I'd rather have you for strength than anybody else I know of; but I can't keep 'round after you all the time. I shouldn't hired you when I did, only I was in a tight place for help, and you happened along."

"Ain't you satisfied?" asked the young man.

"Yes," was the reply. "Hain't I told you so? If I hain't, I meant to. But you know what a name you've got, both sides of the river; and, to-day, I've heard something about your running off with Duke Moran's girl. Where is she? Do you know anything about her?"

"I'll tell you all about that," said Tom hoarsely, a desire to exonerate himself from undeserved blame struggling with his anger.

His companion looked at him keenly while he was speaking, occasionally asking a question, which was answered with apparent truthfulness. "I don't quite understand it," was the only comment.

"I don't neither," responded the young man. "I can't tell what made me want to take her home; only I was afraid there'd be a row about my hurting her, and there wouldn't nobody have her."

"You've kept clear of liquor since then?"

"Yes, and mean to for the present."

"Then come again to-morrow, and I'll find work for you as long as you keep sober. Want your pay to-night?"

"Yes. If you pay me, the old man won't get it, and I won't work to have him take my wages. I'll spend what I earn as I'm a mind to."

Only part of his wages was spent that evening; he carrying the remainder to Patsy Quinn, who engaged to keep it safely until he should call for it. His father had been to Lion's Mouth, and threatened violence if his wife did not return home; but her guardian answered threat with threat, and the miserable drunkard went on his lonely way, with manners somewhat subdued.

"Good for you, Patsy!" cried the young man, laughing at his father's discomfiture. "I hope the old man learnt a lesson he'll remember."

"He'll be back," said Mrs. Magee sadly. "I'm expecting him every minute. I hope you won't go away?"

"But I must," was the reply. "I've promised to go to a good place; and I must. Patsy knows about it, and she says go."

"Yes, I do. I can take care of things here. I want you to look as well as you can, so, after supper, you'll find some clean clothes in the bedroom."

So many thinking of his happiness! So many looking to him for assistance! Little Kate Moran welcomed him with a smile, reaching out her thin hand to touch him as he passed her. She had read the book given him by Wilbur Richards — read it aloud, as well as she was able, and then pored over it to learn the words which, at first, seemed too hard for her. Child as she was, she was far wiser in some ways than her companions. She had a simple, loving faith in God as the Father of all, both rich and poor. She knew that Christ came into the world to make atonement for sin, and that whosoever believeth on him shall be saved.

"You don't mean to say that God loves everybody?" remarked Patsy Quinn, when, in answer to some question, she had asserted this fundamental doctrine of Christianity.

"My mother said so, and she knew,"

was Kate's reply. "And there's a verse in the Bible says so, too. Mother had me say it ever so many times, so I shouldn't forget it. I'll say it now: "God so loved the world, that he gave his only-begotten Son, that whosoever believeth on him might not perish, but have everlasting life.' The 'world' means everybody, and 'Son' means Jesus. He's the one 'that died. Mother had a Bible; but father sold it, and I never had one since. The first money I earn, I mean to buy one."

If ever Mrs. Quinn felt the awe inspired by holy fear, it was then. Years before, she had hidden her Bible in the depths of an old chest which she seldom opened; and there, beneath heaps of rubbish, it lay, with all its blessed truths unheeded. When the Bible was thus banished from her presence, she had been fain to curse God and die; but some impulse restrained her from self-destruction, and gradually life grew to be less irksome. Now, although she did not care to hear more of God and Jesus, she brought forward her Bible, and placed it in the hands of the child.

"Why, it's just like mother's, with just such pictures, and just such a cover!" exclaimed Kate. "May I read it all I want to?"

"Yes, to be sure," was the reply. "You can have it for your own while you stay with me."

Tom Magee fancied that his little charge looked very bright and happy; but he did not guess the reason; indeed, his own personal interests so engrossed his thoughts that others received small attention. When supper was eaten, and the clean clothes examined, he in some measure appreciated the kindness of his humble friend. He hesitated before appropriating the articles which her son had worn, and which she must have treasured almost sacredly; but a word decided him; and presently he appeared with immaculate shirt front, wristbands, and collar.

"You'll do," remarked Patsy, surveying him from head to foot. "Now, mind all you hear, and do as you're told. You'd better work for Mis Richards' folks for half-pay than work for anybody else. You needn't worry about anything here. I guess I can take care of my own house."

"Don't you think he'll come?" asked Wilbur Richards, looking up anxiously into his mother's face.

"I hope so, my son," she answered. "It is hardly time for him yet."

A piano occupied a recess of the room in which mother and son were sitting, and to while away an hour of waiting the latter ran his fingers carelessly over the keys. The sweet chords thrilled his heart; and, responsive to his touch, a grand burst of music filled the room, while his whole nature felt its subduing power, and he continued to play until fatigue obliged him to desist. As he turned from the instrument, he encountered the fixed gaze of Tom

Magee, who, having been shown into the room, and motioned to a seat, neither moved nor spoke.

"Good-evening! I'm glad to see you," said the musician. And his companion, after drawing a long sigh of satisfaction, replied by a simple "Good-evening."

"Have you been here long, my friend?"

"I don't know, sir. I never should know about the time, if I could hear such music as you made."

"Then you like it. I'm glad of that, because it shows that we have some tastes in sympathy. I suppose you have been hard at work all day?"

"Yes, sir."

"And are you very tired?"

"No, sir; I ain't often tired."

"How happy you ought to be! It seems to me I should be perfectly happy, if I had as much strength as you have."

"But I can't make any music with my fingers," said Tom, glancing at his brown hands. "I don't see how you do it."

"It's easy, like everything else, when you know how," was the reply. "I presume you could learn to make music; but it wouldn't be the best way for you to spend your time."

"No, 'twouldn't. I've something else to do. I must earn money," said the visitor, who was ill at ease in the well-furnished room, although alone with Wilbur Richards.

"Be thankful that you have strength to earn money," was the response. "You are rich."

"Oh! no, sir. I'm very poor. I haven't got a dollar in the world, nor a suit of decent clothes. I was ashamed to come here to-night, but I wanted to. And, besides, you said you wanted somebody to work for you."

"Yes, I do. But perhaps you'll be disappointed when you hear what kind of work I want done. I want somebody to do good for me."

"Then I won't answer, sir, and I'd better be going," murmured poor Tom. "You knew I couldn't do that," he added, in a reproachful tone.

"I know you *can*, if you *will*," said his companion, laying one hand lightly upon his shoulder. "And *I* will do *you* good, if you will allow me. Come, my friend, we are both of us young; just beginning in the world, and we can help each other. We have been strangers, but we have started on the same journey, and are bound for the same place." A look of surprise on the visitor's face was equivalent to a question, which was answered quickly. "We are going to the judgment-seat of God, you and I, to be judged for the deeds done here in the body."

Tom Magee had always scoffed at religion, at churches, at the Bible, and at every mention of things holy. Now, however, when this impressive truth was spoken by one so far above him in social position, and under circumstances so novel, he felt no inclination to scoff or sneer. He knew not how to reply; but after much effort, he succeeded in expressing his embarrassment: "You hain't lived as I have," he said, in conclusion. "You don't know how I've lived."

"No, I dont'; but, if you wished to tell me, I might help you to a better way of living, my friend. I have not lived as I ought. Every one does wrong, some in one way, and some in another. You know that."

"I never thought. I should guess, though, that you always done right."

"Then you would guess wrong," said Wilbur Richards with great seriousness. "I am a sinner like yourself."

"No, not like me, sir. That can't be. You never got drunk, or took what don't belong to you, or got into a row, or said bad words. I'm sure you hain't done such things, and I have; so we ain't alike."

"But we are both sinners in the sight of

God, my friend; and, if we ever get to heaven, it will be because Christ died for us. You understand that?"

"I don't know," answered poor Tom, sadly bewildered by the conversation of his host. At one moment he was tempted to leave the house without excuse or ceremony; the next, he longed to tell this new friend all his troubles and perplexities. Angry with himself, and yet unable to resist the influence of one who looked into his eyes with such loving earnestness, he could only return the gaze with one of unfeigned astonishment. "I don't know much about anything good," he added.

"You can learn," was the reply. "You know you *must* learn, if you are going to do my work. I lie here on the couch for whole days, and think what I would do if I was well and strong. I never tell mother what I am thinking, because it would trouble her, and she has trouble enough with me now. May I tell you?"

"Yes, sir," replied the still wondering visitor; "I'd be glad to have you."

"I would help everybody that's in trouble. If any one had a heavy load to carry, I would take part of it. I saw an old man go past here, the other day, with a full basket, and I wanted to help *him*. He trembled as he walked. You could have helped him."

"Yes, sir."

"Then there is one way you could do good, if you were on the lookout for opportunities."

"Yes, sir; but, you see, I'd been more likely to give him a push." And a flush of shame overspread the speaker's face, as he remembered how often his strength had been exerted to the injury of others. "That's what I've always done; but I guess I've hurt myself most of anybody. I never've done any good in all my life, unless it's been these two days since I went to work. I hain't drinked a drop of liquor."

"That is well! That is beginning in the right way. Now, if I can help you along, I shall be very glad to do so. Suppose I tell you something about myself, so you may feel better acquainted with me."

Assured that this would be welcome, Wilbur Richards commenced by speaking of his childhood. Even then he was an invalid, suffering so much from pain and weariness that he could seldom join in the sports of more robust children. When he was ten years of age, his father had died. He lingered over this sad experience, describing the last days of one whom he had well-nigh worshipped, and repeating the last words which had enjoined him to be found faithful in his allotted work.

"You loved your father," said Tom softly.

"Certainly I did. He was worthy of love. I used to think he was perfect; and now it seems to me he was as nearly so as any one can be. If I am ever as good as he was, I shall be satisfied."

"I guess I'd been better if I'd had such a father." These words escaped the visitor; and, as his companion waited for further comment, he added: "You don't know what 'tis to have such a father as mine is."

"No, my friend, I don't. I'm sorry for you. There's the making of a noble man in you. Perhaps no one has ever told you that before; but I am sure of it. O Tom Magee! you ought to be one of the best men in the country!" And in his enthusiasm, the speaker clasped the hard, brown hand of his companion. "Put back your hair from your forehead, and let me see how you would look at your best."

"'Twon't stay back," was the reply. "It's just like a mop."

"A handsome mop," replied Wilbur Richards, with a smile, as Tom threaded his fingers through the masses of dark, curly hair, and revealed a broad, full forehead. "Regular brushing would keep it in place; and as for the curls, you can't afford to lose them."

After all his thought and anxiety in regard to this interview, the young man, so anxious to accomplish some good, had not followed his proposed plan. Standing on common ground, he sought to establish a bond of good-fellowship, rather than inpress his visitor with a sense of his own superiority. His genial manners and hearty words produced the desired effect. The barriers of reserve were broken down; and once commencing a history of his past life, Tom Magee spoke rapidly and truthfully.

"You see how 'tis," he said, in conclusion. "There's the old man, so bad he couldn't be worse; and there's mother, all broken down and afraid of her life; and there's little Kate, that I've promised to take care of. What's to be done?"

"The best you can, my friend. I'll tell you what I think I should do, if I was in your place."

"I wish you would," was the reply. "I don't seem to keep to one mind long at a time, and I'll be glad to hear you."

"Well, Tom—I want to speak that name once—I would call my father 'father,' not the 'old man.' I would provide for my mother, if hard work could do it. I don't know exactly what to say about that child. It is no place for her in your home, and I am afraid Mrs. Quinn is not the best woman in the world to bring her up. Is Mrs. Quinn a Christian?"

"No, sir, I guess not. I don't know really what you mean. She don't go to meeting Sundays, but she's always ready to do anybody a good turn, and she's down on liquor. You see, she's reason for that. Katy knows about God. She told me, and she read the book you gave. I read some of it. I'll read the rest, and—and—I'll try not to say 'old man' again."

"That is right! Try to do your father some good. Perhaps you can make him a better man. I think I would try if I was well and strong as you are."

"How would you begin?" No wonder Tom asked this hopelessly.

"I'd set him a good example," was the reply. "Be a thorough-going temperance man, as I am now. A few weeks ago, I consulted a physician, who advised me to drink Bourbon whiskey. He said it would tone up my system, and give me strength; but I don't believe it, and if I did I wouldn't drink the vile stuff three months if I knew it would add ten years to my life. I won't die a drunkard!"

"But you wouldn't be a drunkard if you only took it regular, every day. Folks that do that ain't drunkards."

"What are they, then?"

"I don't know. Something besides drunkards."

"Well, my friend, I know. They are the material out of which drunkards are made by the wholesale—moderate drinkers. How do I know I could leave off my whiskey at the end of three months?"

"You could if you was a mind to."

"But people say the appetite for liquor

increases with indulgence, until a man has no power to abstain from it."

"I don't believe that," was Tom's reply. "I suppose a man'd hanker after it, and feel dry, but he'd be a fool if he couldn't hold on. I think likely I've drinked as much liquor as any boy of my age; but I needn't drink another drop unless I'm a mind to. I know that."

"I'm glad to hear you say so, my friend, and I'm sure you speak the truth," Wilbur Richards responded. "I know you have a strong will. If you should once decide to abandon all your bad habits, you would do so."

"What's the use?"

"The use! Wouldn't you rather live in a good house than a poor one? Wouldn't you rather be respected than despised, and wouldn't you rather go to heaven than be shut out?"

"Yes, sir." These two words, breathed rather than spoken, expressed far more than a simple assent. Sitting there, contrasting his own wretched home with that in which he was now a guest, Tom Magee realized his degradation as never before. In his way, he had been a king among his fellows; praised for his strength and recklessness, consulted in every emergency, and feared when he chose to assert authority. After all, he was only a boy, as Patsy had said, and it was natural that these things should have weight with him. He looked at his present companion—the pale, spiritual face, fine intellectual head, and slight figure. How far his inferior in physical force, and yet how far above him in all which constitutes true superiority!

Neither seemed disposed to break the silence. One was too wise to do this; the other, too much engrossed with his own thoughts. At length, young Richards walked across the room, and summoned to his aid the spirit of music.

"I think I'd better go, now," said his

guest, as he turned from the piano. "Thank you, sir, for all you've said, and I'll try to remember."

"And you'll come again?"

"Yes, sir, if you want me to."

"I do want you to, my friend; and, if you need any help, come to me. If I can't help you in one way, perhaps I can in another. It sometimes does us good to talk of our troubles, and I am sure I shall want help. My mother will call upon Mrs. Quinn and your mother, if you think they would like to see her. You'll be sure to come again?" added the speaker with a wistful look.

"Yes, sir; I shall want to come, if I don't go back to the old way."

"O Tom! you won't do that. It seems as though you couldn't while I'm praying for you. What shall you do next Sabbath?"

"I don't know."

"Will you come here, for an hour or

two, in the afternoon? Come, whether you go back or not."

There was some hesitation on the part of him who was thus addressed; but at last the desired promise was given, and Tom left the house. As he went out, he bared his head to the night wind, pushed back the clustering curls from his brow, and strode on, up the lonely path which followed the windings of the river. At Lion's Mouth a gleaming light gave him mute welcome, but he continued his walk till he reached the old hut. Here he heard groans which proceeded from his father, and asked quickly, "What's the matter?"

An oath prefaced the answer, "I've broke my leg." Another oath. "I dragged myself into the house before dark, and here I've laid. Why didn't you come home in decent season?"

"I didn't mean to come at all," was the reply. "I don't know what made me come, but I'm glad I did."

"I'm glad, too," said the prostrate man, with a fearfully profane imprecation. "I've got to have the doctor. Give me that bottle out of the cupboard. There's victuals and drink in that. Take a swig yourself, and pass it along."

"No, father; I won't take a swig myself, and I won't give it to you. You've had enough, and I don't want it. I'll light a candle if I can find one, and then go after Dr. Hibbard. There wouldn't no city doctor come here to-night."

"I don't want no city doctor. Give me the bottle, and start along."

A candle was lighted, and Tom started for the short walk across the fields to Dr. Hibbard's house. The doctor was at home; but there was some delay on his part, and some hesitation to taking charge of a patient where there seemed no prospect of remuneration. This matter, however, settled, he promised to "be right along."

Upon his return, the young man found

his father nearly crazed with thirst and rage. He was swearing at his son when the doctor arrived, and from this medical gentleman he received sympathy. Search was made for the bottle, but it had vanished. There was no liquor in the house; neither would any be furnished in response to his demands. Jim Magee expended a vast deal of breath to no purpose; and, dismissing Dr. Hibbard with an oath, when told there was nothing for him to do but keep still, he tried the power of persuasion. It was pitiful to listen to him, so abject were his pleadings, so terrible his sufferings; yet to all came the answer, "No, father."

"But I'm burning up. I shall die without."

"Then die, and be—" The terrible word was unspoken.

"I hain't had nothing to eat since morning—not a mouthful—and I'm starving. You want me to die?"

"Why shouldn't I?" asked the son involuntarily. "You hain't ever done me any good. I'd be better off if you was to die." Then, remembering the advice of Wilbur Richards, he added, "I'll bring you something to eat."

"You ain't going to leave me alone, Tom? Don't! I can't stay alone."

"Then you'll have to go without anything to eat. There ain't anything in the house."

"I know it," was said, with a groan.

"Well, go along. Tell your mother I want her. If she don't come, I'll make her sorry for it."

Without hearing the last order, he hastened away, and presently was relating such particulars of the accident as he had been able to learn.

"And you had Dr. Hibbard to set the leg," said Patsy Quinn. "Then it's likely to me the job'll have to be done over, or the old man'll be a cripple for life. The doctor ain't sober no time after dinner, but he's good as his patient." While saying this, the woman bustled about, collecting such provision from Tom's supplies as she thought might be needed at the hut, and then volunteered to go there herself. "No, Mis Magee, don't you think of going," she exclaimed. "It's no place for you, to-night. Wait till I come back." Out-of-doors, she turned to her companion with the question, "What kind of work does Wilbur Richards want you to do?"

"He wants me to do good for him—help everybody I can, and make something of myself," was the reply.

"Is that all, Tom?"

"All!" was repeated sharply. "That's enough. You'd think· so if you'd heard him talk. I don't know what I'm going to do, but I'm going there again, next Sunday. He knows most everything that I don't. He had a good father, and the old man—there, that's wrong. He said 'twas. Patsy, do you know anything about heaven?"

"Not much," she answered sadly. "I used to hear about it when I was a girl; and Katy's been talking about it to-day. Did he talk about it?"

"Yes, and he's going there, sure. Wonder if there's any place for such a boy as I've been? There's something new the matter with me. I don't know what 'tis, but I mean to try—" He did not finish this sentence, and perhaps his companion did not need that he should do so. She comprehended his silence.

Solitude had not improved the temper of Jim Magee, as he soon gave evidence. He still demanded liquor, swore he would have it, and closed his tirade with a frightful howl of rage. To all this, his son made no response beyond reiterating previous refusals, and adding a needed caution as to quiet.

Patsy moved noiselessly about the kitchen, preparing such nourishment as the drunkard's condition required. This accomplished, she held a whispered consultation with Tom, after which she went home, where she exerted her utmost powers of persuasion to induce Mrs. Magee to remain with her. Fortunately, she was successful; but the poor woman, half-crazed with fear and tortured with anxiety, could only count the lagging hours and long for morning.

No rest, either, had her son. In after-years, he was accustomed to speak of that night as a night of horrors. What with the ravings of his father, the accusations of his conscience, and the keen sense of degradation which he endured, the night answered to an eternity of time. Was this weary watching part of the work he was to do for Wilbur Richards? Was his father stricken down as the first step toward reform?

With only the stars above him while he paced to and fro before the hut, these and kindred questions thronged his mind. When time to make preparations for leaving his father, he said, "Mother'll come and stay with you, to-day, if you'll treat her decent."

"You going off?" was the reply.

"Of course I am. You want a fire and something to eat. How do you expect you can have anything, if I don't work for it? I'll spend my wages for you now; but, if you was well, you shouldn't have a cent, and now you sha'n't have any for liquor."

"Want all the liquor for yourself?" answered Jim Magee, in a sneering tone.

"No, I don't," said the young man, after a moment's silence, in which he strove to obtain the mastery over himself. "I hain't drinked a drop this four days; and I sha'n't again, just yet. I've got enough to do without that. If you want mother to stay with you to-day, she'll come; but you'll stay alone to-morrow, if I hear of any trouble."

I will not describe the incidents of this day, or of those which succeeded it, until Tom found himself due at a meeting of "The Owls." To meet his engagement was not pleasant; to forfeit it would be inconsistent with both his past character and present intentions. The Sabbath interview with Wilbur Richards had greatly strengthened him; yet there would be much to test his moral courage. His old companions would in every possible way tempt him to return to them. It was late when he went to the room which had been the scene of so many carousals, and, giving the password, was admitted. The veritable owl which winked and blinked in his wire cage wore not a more impenetrable aspect than did the young man who seated himself silently at a table. His appearance forbade any uproarious greeting.

"The Big Owl must give an account of himself." No response was made, and again these words were repeated.

At this Tom sprang to his feet, and for the next ten minutes proceeded to give such an account of himself as his listeners did not care to hear: "I demand that you release me from all my promises, and count me out of your number," he said, in conclusion. "'Tain't no use if you don't. I won't come to no more of your meetings, and I won't have nothing to do with your scrapes. I wish you'd all give up. We've come pretty nigh the wind a good many times, and you're sure to get into trouble."

"We won't give up ourselves, and we won't give you up," muttered one.

"You'll do that last," was the reply. "You can't bully me. I'm bound to do as I'm a mind to."

If anything had been needed to confirm Tom in his decision to cut loose from the company of those around him, it was supplied by the opposition he encountered. A fair-haired boy, whose restless movements had not been unobserved while he was speaking, came near to him, saying in a low tone, "I want to go with you."

"Is that so, Jack? Then you shall, and I'll help you get clear from this set."

Cries of "No, you don't," mingled with oaths, resounded through the room, until Tom Magee, in an authoritative voice, commanded silence, adding, "Hear what more I've got to say."

Up to this time, no liquor had been drunk. Now all hands proposed a drink.

"Take a glass of something, Tom, and then we'll hear you. You're getting dry. We're all dry. There's Jack needs a thorough wetting."

A glass passed to Jack's lips was dashed to the floor, and a strong arm thrown around him. "I don't never want to drink any more," he said. "It 'most kills mother to have me, and I know its awful mean. But they'll make me."

"No, they won't," answered Tom decidedly, as he remembered how he had helped to drag down this boy to the same level with himself. I'll stand by you. You'd better go home, and leave me to fight it out alone," he added, as the strife waxed more bitter. "Slip out the door when I open it, and don't stop for anything till you're safe with your mother. I'll see you within an hour."

So many voices were raised in dispute, so many feet were tramping and shuffling, that these instructions were not overheard. The door had been opened and closed before Jack's intention was suspected, and then his friend prevented any attempt to follow him.

"Well, now, Tom, if you're going to leave us, just drink one glass to show you don't bear us no ill-will. Let's all sit down, and talk the matter over, without such a row. 'Tain't no way, and I don't like it."

A brimming glass of liquor without dilution was pushed towards Tom Magee, who found the fumes appealing to his senses in a manner which threatened his powers of resistance. Retreat seemed the better part of valor; yet he remained long enough to reiterate once more his determination, and answer some enquiries, made partly in good faith, and partly in derision.

"Now I'm going, and stop me who dares!" he exclaimed at last. "If any of you want help to do better, come to me; but just remember, I ain't no Owl."

CHAPTER III.

THE STRONGEST AND THE VILEST MUST OWN GOD'S SOVEREIGN POWER.

HE ungrammatical assertion with which Tom Magee closed his speech was no offence to the listeners, save in its significance. They had not counted on his persistence in the determination to leave them. Two of their number had withdrawn. *One* would come back, *should* come back; but Tom was a stubborn fact, not easily managed.

Jack Wetherbee had hastened home to the upper room, where, after, a hard day's work in the mill, his mother was busily sewing. Thinking of her boy, the needle dropped from her nerveless fingers, as she cried involuntarily, "O God! lay not this burden upon me. I cannot bear it!" She had borne poverty, had seen the grave close over the form of a kind, loving husband, and yet had not murmured. But now, a heavier burden, a keener sorrow, had threatened her, and in agony of spirit she cried to God for deliverance. As many a mother has done, and, alas! as many a mother shall do, while strong drink claims its victims, she prayed for death rather than life.

And yet her boy loved her. There were times when he promised reformation, and talked of all he would do when he was a man. Only fourteen years of age, and reform as necessary for him as for any gray-haired sinner!

It may have been ill-judged on the part of Mrs. Wetherbee to keep him with her, when, from early morning till the evening was well-nigh spent, she could only see him for a short half-hour. She might have found a home for him in some farmer's family; but where, then, would her own home be? "I must take him with me," she had said to the friends who urged her to leave Jackson in the country, and for a time she saw no reason to regret her decision. Then for months hope alternated with fear, yet she would not send him from her.

He knew his duty, regretted his weakness in yielding to evil companionship, and was overwhelmed with shame whenever he reflected upon his conduct. A fortnight before the evening in question, he had been so intoxicated that his mother threatened him with banishment from her presence if he offended again in like manner. Sometimes he wished to go away where he would not be tempted to do wrong; but his mother, wiser than he, knew that he must learn to resist temptation if he would be truly good. She prayed for him, wept over him, and, mother-like, loved him all the more for the tears she shed and the prayers she uttered.

A man whose family occupied the lower rooms of the house in which she lived, and who watched Jack's career with interest, had advised her to "get him out of the city as soon as possible. There's trouble brewing for the set he's been with," said the man. "They're getting well known; and, if anything happens, Jack'll come in for his share of the blame."

Mrs. Wetherbee was thinking of this when a hurried step on the stairs announced the coming of her son. Without speaking, he threw himself upon his knees beside her, and buried his face in her lap. He had not been drinking. She saw that at a glance; and, thankful as she was, asked no questions. There was a rap on the door of her room. "Come in," she said, and Tom Magee crossed the threshold. Instinctively she threw one arm around her boy, while she waited for her visitor to make known his business.

"I've come to see Jack."

At these words Jack sprang to his feet, exclaiming, "Did you mean what you said, to-night?"

"I did mean just that," was the earnest reply.

"You won't never drink any more liquor?"

Tom hesitated a moment. He had not taken the pledge of total abstinence; was not certain that he should do so. He didn't like the idea of too many promises, although he had never objected to them when they bound him to an evil course. Mrs. Wetherbee looked at him beseechingly. Jack held his hand, gazing up into his face as though everything depended upon what he should say.

"I never'll drink another drop of liquor as long as I live, so help me God! Are you ready to say that, Jack?"

"Yes, I am," was the response. And again the solemn pledge was repeated.

"What does all this mean?" now asked Mrs. Wetherbee. "I don't understand. Ain't you Tom Magee?"

"Yes, ma'am; but I ain't the same I was

two weeks ago. 'Twas me got Jack back to drinking, last time; but I'm going to help him leave off now. I can't stop to tell you all about it, but I'll tell some." And, speaking rapidly, he gave a general outline of the events which had wrought such a change in his habits. "I've been one of the worst," he said in conclusion. "I'm trying to do better now, but I've got a hard row to hoe. I can help Jack, though, if the others bully him. May be you'd like some of these tracts," he said, after a short silence; and, taking a package from his pocket, he gave Mrs. Wetherbee a liberal supply. "They're some a young man that's sick wanted I should give away for him. If you want anything of me, Jack, leave word at Lion's Mouth, and I'll be on hand. You can trust Patsy."

"Guess I've done one job for Wilbur Richards, to-night," soliloquized Tom, as he hurried through the streets, across the bridge, and up the river path. "Who'd thought of my turning tract-peddler!" Ten o'clock.

Too late for any call on his way. His mother must be relieved from her weary watch.

"I'm so glad you've come," she said joyfully. "I was afraid."

"No wonder, mother; though there wasn't nothing to be afraid of for me. I'm all right. Now, go up-stairs, and sleep like a top, if you know how that is."

It was no easy task to care for Jim Magee in his helplessness, although a wholesome fear of consequences restrained him from savage outbreaks. He was provided with everything necessary for his comfort. Nothing was denied him except the liquor which he most craved; and this it was impossible for him to obtain. His old associates kept aloof from him. Dr. Hibbard would not provide it unless sure of remuneration. Tom, who had taken occasion to say that he would never pay for a drop of the poison stuff, wished to dismiss the tippling doctor and call in another; but his father swore that no other should darken the doors.

Meanwhile, enquiries were made for Kate Moran. In one of his rounds, Tom was accosted by a respectable-looking woman, who asked him if he could tell her anything about Duke Moran's little girl.

"Yes, ma'am," he answered. "I can tell you that she has a good home, and is well taken care of."

"Where?"

"At Lion's Mouth, the other side of the river. She lives with a poor woman; but she'll have what she needs, and there needn't anybody worry about her."

The woman looked at Tom a little suspiciously as she said: "I'd like to go and see her. I used to know her mother when we were girls. I heard she went off with you, after you threw a stone that hurt her arm."

"Yes, ma'am, she did. I didn't mean to hurt her, and I don't know what made me take her with me, only I was afraid there'd be trouble. I wish you *would* go and see her; she'll be glad to see you if you knew her mother. She don't seem to have many friends."

"She's got relations enough, uncles, aunts, and cousins, plenty of them; but, you see, they wouldn't have anything to do with her mother after she married Duke. He was smart, but he was poor; and they wanted her to marry a rich man, as she might. Then, when Duke took to drinking as he did, they acted as though she never belonged to them. I used to work at her father's, so I know all about it."

"Yes, ma'am," replied Tom, not quite sure whether he was glad or sorry that there were those who had a right to claim Kate Moran. A week before, he would have been angry at the very thought of this; now, he was beginning to realize how much depended upon her proper training and education. Mrs. Richards had visited the child with the intention of offering her a home, yet leaving her without doing so.

"Little Kate is doing a good work," remarked the lady, upon her return. "At present, it is best for her and all concerned that she should remain where she is."

"But, mother, she needs to be taught many things she can never learn at Mrs. Quinn's," was urged in reply.

"Perhaps so; but for this winter she is in the right place. Six months may work a wondrous change."

"Yes, mother, six months will work a wondrous change in the natural world. The earth will have put on her beautiful garment. Flowers will blossom, and birds sing. I wish I could believe that the moral change in our new friends will be as great."

"Are you losing faith?" asked Mrs. Richards smilingly.

"Oh! no," was the cheerful reply. "I am only a little disappointed; but I shall soon forget it. I can wait six months for the fulfilment of my hopes."

"Do you know what your hopes really are, Wilbur?"

"In a general way, mother. They will take a more definite form as they tend to fulfilment. I know that I hope all things good for Tom Magee."

So did the poor fellow hope for himself; although he was thinking and hoping nearly as much for others as for himself. Jackson Wetherbee, to whom he seemed as a tower of strength, waited for him at street-corners, just to hear an encouraging word or catch a genial smile. "All right?" was a question sometimes asked, to be answered by the same phrase differently emphasized, while the two passed on, each his own way.

Every morning, Tom went to the wood-yard: every evening, he carried to his poor home some needed comfort; carried, also, a softened heart and improved manners. His calls were short at Lion's Mouth, shorter than he would have desired; yet he found opportunities to tell Patsy Quinn whatever she desired to know of his welfare. Kate Moran's interests were discussed with great earnestness.

"It don't seem as though I could get along without her," said the woman. "I'd be willing to work a good deal harder for the sake of havin' her around. It don't seem to cost anything to keep her. Mis Richards give her some clothes, and I'm going to do the rest. You've got enough on your hands without her. The old man's going to be a bill of expense, and he can't help it if he wants to. Your mother's got to have something to wear. Wait till I've got through!" now exclaimed the speaker, eager to meet all objections to her plans before they were uttered. "You've got some back rent to pay on the old place; and you want some provisions in the cellar, now it's banked up. Your mother told me how hard you worked nights to do that. You're a good boy, Tom, if I do say it to your face. I wouldn't believed you'd made the kitchen look so well with the new paper. 'Twas a bright thought in you, instead of covering the cracks with newspapers. You make the money you earn go a good ways."

"Yes; and that's just the reason I can do something for Kate," replied Tom quickly.

"But you want some new clothes for yourself," was the response. "You'll want to go to meeting Sundays. Your mother's took to mending; but you'll want one decent suit without patches. And there's the doctor's bill. Your mother's talking about trying to earn some money."

"She won't do it while I can work," said the young man decidedly. "She's got enough to do at home; and if she can't be comfortable there, I'll complain of father, and have him shut up. I've told him so, and I'll do as I say. 'Twould be better for him than living as he has the last five years."

"Yes, Tom, 'most anything's better'n

that. It's been hard living up your way; and now it don't seem possible that you're the same lad that went swearing about, drunk half the time, and likely to get into all kinds of scrapes. You mean to hold out, don't you?"

"I've got to, Patsy. I've took the oath, and that means something to me now. But I'm most wild when I think of all that's happened. I've helped pull down so many other boys, just for the sake of seeing what I could do. And—and—there's something else, Patsy. I'm afraid of God. Did you ever feel afraid of God?"

"I don't know, Tom. I don't think much about God. Leastways I didn't till since Katy come here. She talks about him, and says she loves him. She ain't afraid of him."

"No more should she be. What's she ever done to make her afraid? It's because I'm so wicked. When I read the tracts, sometimes I want to burn them all up, and I most hate God. Then I'm ready to get down on my knees, and ask him to forgive me for everything I've done that's wrong. I do believe I'd do that if I could see him as I see you, and I'd hold on to him till he answered me one way or another. It's so strange that we can't never be out of his sight, when we can't see him. It's dreadful wicked, but I've wished lately, a good many times, that there wa'n't any God."

Tom Magee said this last under his breath, as though it was of some strange thing he spoke; and yet his was not an unusual experience. When first the sinner feels his utter helplessness to atone for past wrong-doing—feels, also, the presence of an offended God, whom he has no power to propitiate, he is fain to wish that such a God did not exist. The sinful heart rebels; and as with each succeeding hour of serious thought the burden of guilt presses more heavily, conflicting emotions struggle for the mastery.

This young man, whose ignorance of spiritual things was no greater than that of many another, was just awaking from a lifelong lethargy. How he loathed himself as wholly vile! "I ain't done no good all my life," he said, in his homely way. He didn't mind making this acknowledgment to Patsy, from whom he had never cared to conceal his wickedness.

"But you'll do better now, and that'll make it all right. So don't fret over it," was the reply of his friend.

"That won't help what's 'ready done, Patsy. You see, if all the things are wrote down against me in a book somewhere, I can't rub them out."

"Wrote down! What do you mean by that? Who wrote them?"

"God," answered Tom solemnly. "That's what Wilbur Richards told me, and he knows."

"Yes, he knows," echoed Patsy. "But it don't seem as though it could be. You don't suppose every word we speak, and every single little thing we do, is wrote down, do you?"

"He said so; and all we think, too; so there ain't no way of getting rid of it. It's hard, ain't it, for such a boy as I've been?"

"I'm 'most a mind not to believe it, if he did say so," exclaimed the poor woman.

"But he says it's in the Bible," was Tom's response. "The Bible's all true. Katy knows about it. You ask her, and she'll tell you more."

"Seems to me I don't want to hear no more. I'm just as wicked as you be, Tom; and perhaps I'm wickeder. May be, if I'd always done right, things wouldn't be as they are now. Do try and be good now, my lad, and not break your mother's heart. Poor woman! She's had a hard time; but she's better off now. I know that, and I'm glad of it. We're all better off since you found Katy."

"Yes; good-night. Mother'll be expecting me."

Mother had something new to display that evening. A bit of a rug which she had braided at odd times lay before the stove, and gave quite an air of comfort to the room.

"It's nice-looking, and the floor's clean, and we've got a good fire and a good supper," said Tom, enumerating their comforts. "I wouldn't be put back where we was six weeks ago, for a pile of money."

"I'd rather die," responded Mrs. Magee earnestly. "I'd gone on that way long as I could."

"Well, mother, we won't go that way any more. I've said it, and I'll stick to it. There's one way, if there ain't another. There won't much more liquor come into this old shell while we live in it, and there won't none of my wages be spent at the grog-shop."

The father heard this in the little bed-room to which he was still confined, and gnashed his teeth in impotent rage. He could not understand Tom. There was something strange about the boy, and, angry as he was at the authority to which he was forced to submit, he could not but respect it. If there had ever been anything like tenderness in his nature, it could not fail now to give some token of its existence; and, truth to tell, there were times when his manner was slightly subdued, and the tones of his voice less harsh than usual.

When Tom read aloud to his mother, his father listened. Indeed the drunkard could not well do otherwise, and listening, he could not but reflect upon what he heard. One evening, after so long a silence that he half fancied himself dreaming, some bitter words spoken by Tom rang in his ear with startling emphasis:

"If there wa'n't nobody but you and I, mother, there'd be a chance for us. I don't hate father as I used to, but I can't make it seem right that I should be kept down by him. Wilbur Richards says his father was 'most perfect, and likely that's what makes him so good. I ain't to blame for father's being a drunkard, but it's just like a stone round my neck, now I'm trying to do better. I feel it all the time."

"Don't be discouraged," was all poor Mrs. Magee could say, although her heart was full of pity and sorrow for her son.

"I ain't discouraged, mother. I'm going ahead," said Tom resolutely. "If I was a Christian, I shouldn't care for anything else. If I was sure God would forgive all my sins, I'd be willing to work night and day. All these tracts say that's the first thing to be thought of, and I believe it."

"O Tom! you find out the way, and tell me," exclaimed his mother. "I want to have *my* sins forgiven, too. If I could feel like some you read about, 'twouldn't make no difference about other things. You find out how 'tis, won't you?"

What could he say but "yes"? What could he do but repeat the instructions he had himself received? Wilbur Richards had told him that he must pray.

"Have you ever prayed, Tom?"

"I've tried, mother; but I made poor work."

"And, oh! Tom, did you ask for me, too?"

"I tried; and I asked God to make father better, too."

A sigh of relief escaped the poor woman as she looked wistfully at her son, as though from him was to come all her help and her salvation. "I found some leaves of an old Testament in the lower bureau drawer, to-day, and I read them all through."

"I didn't know there was any in the house."

"I didn't, either. But it's part of a Testament my Sunday-school teacher give me."

"Did you ever go to Sunday-school?" asked Tom, with much surprise.

"Only a little while," she answered. "'Twas before I got acquainted with your father. He made fun of such things, and I staid away to please him. 'Twould been better if I hadn't. My teacher was a good woman, and I remember some she said to me, though I hain't thought of it before to-day for a good many years."

Several times, Jim Magee was upon the point of interrupting this conversation; but, warned by the past, he remained silent. Later, when he heard Tom praying, in low whispered words, his astonishment was unbounded. His boy praying! "Getting pious! 'Twouldn't last long." He was sure of that.

Others were of the same opinion in regard to the young man who had so suddenly and so strangely abandoned his old habits. Even Wilbur Richards feared a return to dissipation and idleness, notwithstanding the repeated assurances he had received. Mr. Riley experienced a new surprise each morning when Tom appeared, ready for the day's work, asking no leave of absence, and shirking no duty. At first, he had watched his assistant closely; now, he was relaxing this watch, and, not hearing complaints from customers, thought himself fortunate in securing such help.

The Owls did not forget Tom. They formed various plans for luring him back to their companionship, all of which failed, and yet they did not despair. If he would drink one glass of liquor, they could accomplish their purpose. At length, fortune seemed to favor them. They met at a fire, worked on the same engine, and together won great praise for their strength and daring.

At such a time, Tom Magee was a host in himself, and on this occasion he did his best. In the excitement of the moment, he forgot everything but present needs and interests. He was thirsty, and, a mug of ale being offered, he drained it to the last drop. His thirst was increased, and it was not until after the second draught that he realized his folly. "My God!" he exclaimed, as the hot blood coursed through his veins, and the old appetite craved indulgence; yet his voice joined in the wild cheers of those about him.

By great exertions, the fire had been staid at a large block, in the basement of which was the most fashionable drinking saloon of the city. Such as Tom Magee were not admitted within its precincts. Only the well dressed and well connected were allowed to enter. No cheap drinks were sold to the poor and ragged. Captain Blood prided himself upon the respectability of his establishment. A young man could frequent his rooms without losing caste in society. The captain himself was genial and smiling; careful of his reputation, and the reputation of others; always speaking of his customers as "fine young men." He was ready at all times to denounce drunkenness, while he manufactured drunkards by the score. During the ten years he had been engaged in his present business, he had seen many a one to whom he had once bowed graciously, degraded to a brutal sot: yet he smiled on, counting his gains, and ensnaring his victims.

On the night in question, he was princely in his hospitality. At least so said the papers of the following day. The firemen were invited to partake of refreshments in his saloon. "Room for all," he cried; and the motley crowd gave way, as one after another wearing the fireman's badge pressed down the granite steps.

Tom Magee went with others. For one hour, at least, he was the peer of many whose social position he had envied. "The boys" complimented him upon the risks he had encountered and the daring he had manifested.

"We lost a plucky fellow when Duke Moran got his sentence; but you'll make his place good," remarked one with an oath. "When he was sober, he'd do the work of two men; and drunk or sober, he was fireproof. He needn't be afraid of anything hotter than he's been through in this world, and come out without being scorched."

A coarse laugh rewarded the speaker, but

Tom did not join in this laugh. The allusion to Duke Moran suggested thoughts of little Kate, of Patsy, of his mother, of Wilbur Richards, and of the solemn oath by which he had pledged himself to total abstinence. He did not stay to hear another word. Forcing his way up the steps, he rushed on, regardless of friend or foe. At length, his name was shouted by Jack Wetherbee, and his steps were arrested.

"Do stop," cried the boy. "I want you to go home with me," was added in a lower tone, as they stood side by side. "Mother's got some hot coffee and oysters. I told her you was working like a tiger, and she thought you'd be hungry. I saw you go into Blood's, and I was real sorry; but you didn't stay?"

"No, I didn't, Jack. 'Tain't no place for me. They'll half of them be drunk before an hour. They'll get started there, and finish off somewhere else. Where've you been? I didn't see you."

"I've been round where I could see you," was the reply. "Come, now, mother's expecting you. I told her you'd come."

"I don't know as it's best," said Tom hesitatingly. "I ought to go home."

"I know, and that's enough," responded Jack. "I bought the oysters with my own money, and mother knows how to cook them tip-top. We'll have supper as good as the rest."

This settled the matter, and Tom turned back. The supper was as good as had been anticipated, and Mrs. Wetherbee was glad to see him. "Better set here than in a worse place," she said. "There'll be a good many mothers anxious about their boys to-night, and I know how to pity them."

"But, mother, you know you needn't worry about me any more," exclaimed her boy, with sparkling eyes. "I can't be coaxed, and I don't mean to give the boys a chance to drive me. Tom, you're growing handsome," he added in the same breath.

"True as the world, you are. I hope I'll be big as you are, and as good."

"I hope you'll be a great deal better. I'm only trying." And Tom blushed at the remembrance of his weakness in drinking the ale which had been offered him. He had not been accustomed to class this with intoxicating liquors, but from its effects he knew it was no drink for him. Thinking of this, and forgetful of his duties as a guest, he sat silent and motionless.

"What's the matter?" asked Jack. "Don't you like oysters and coffee?"

"Of course I do," was the reply. "But I was thinking. I've got into a bad habit of thinking when I ought to be doing something else."

"Why, you think all the time, don't you, Tom? I do, and I can't help it. I don't want to, either, now. I'm so glad and happy, I don't know just what to do with myself. Ain't you happy, Tom?" All this in a breath, and then the boy waited for an answer, which was given after some hesitation.

"Sometimes I am, when I'm working as hard as I can; but I've a good deal to remember that ain't pleasant."

"We all have," now said Mrs. Wetherbee. "Jackson is so light-hearted just now, that he can't look on the dark side. He's getting on finely in school, and he's found a place to work two hours a day, so he feels very independent."

"Yes, sir, I do," added the boy. "Mother hain't told the whole story, either. I get dinner and supper, so she don't have so much to do; and I wash the dishes and sweep the floor. I've got all the tracts laid up that you gave me, though they're pretty much worn out. All the folks in the house have read them. Do have some more oysters and another cup of coffee."

"No; I thank you. I've eaten plenty, and I'm much obliged to you for a nice supper. I must go home, now. Mother'll be anxious. Can I do anything for you, Jack?"

"Guess not. I don't have much trouble. I'm always busy, so the boys don't have a chance at me; and, lately, they don't seem to care."

"I'm glad of that," replied Tom, smiling pleasantly; and then, rising to go, he thanked Mrs. Wetherbee for her kindness.

"You are very welcome to anything I can do for you," she answered. "I shall never forget what you have done for Jack; and now, if you'll stay and visit with him a few minutes, I'll go down-stairs and talk with our neighbors a little."

The visitor wondered at this; but no sooner were they alone than Jack exclaimed, "That's some of my doings. I've got something to tell you, though perhaps it won't make any difference whether you know it or not. The boys are trying to get you into trouble. They've got a new fellow from Boston, and he's up to all sorts of deviltry.

You know there's some tools with your name marked on them, and Rob Morrison says 'twouldn't be strange if they're found somewhere some time, to make folks think you left them. Rob wouldn't told, only because you pulled him out of the river, last summer."

"Much obliged to him," was the reply. "Rob's got a heart if he is bad. Is that all you wanted of me, Jack?"

"No, not quite," answered the boy. "I want you to go to Sabbath-school with me. There's a new class, with only two of us in it, and the teacher says it must be filled up from outside. I want you to come and see if you don't like it. We hear lots of good talking, recite our lessons, and have good books to read."

"I never went to Sabbath-school in my life," said Tom. "I shouldn't know how to behave, and I don't know no more about the Bible than a Hottentot. I couldn't learn the lessons. Your mother helps you, don't she?"

"Yes; wouldn't your mother help you?"

Poor Tom shook his head, saying, "We're all heathen at our house, only for what I've learned lately. Somebody else asked me to go to Sabbath-school, and I'll see about it when I get some decent clothes. Why don't you ask Rob Morrison? His folks belong to the meeting kind. He's got a sister that's a real good woman."

"I *will* ask him," said Jack decidedly. "But you won't get him into trouble for telling?"

"No danger of that," was the reply. "Tell him I'm much obliged, and, if he wants anything of me, he can come over. So can you. Good-night."

The confusion incident to the fire had not subsided when Tom Magee found himself once more in the street. By this time many of the firemen were intoxicated, and, before he crossed the bridge, Tom was called upon to assist two to their homes."

"Ain't drunk yourself, be you?" said one,

who was answered so decidedly that he looked at his companion to assure himself that he was not mistaken in the person. "Heard something about your turning over a new leaf, but thought likely you'd got over it by this time. Got awful dry to-night, didn't you? There'll be a row when I get home. Always is when men folks take a little comfort their own way. Women don't know nothing about it. Tell you, Tom, we must stand up for our rights, and not let 'em git the upper-hand. If they do, they'll keep us dry as a last year's mullen stalk."

Judging by the laughter which greeted this last remark, it must have been considered by some extremely witty, but to Tom it was simply disgusting, and as soon as possible he hastened away.

There was a light in Patsy's window, and, knowing that she would think of him, he stopped long enough to tell her something of the fire, and assure her that he was all right. Nearly the same words said to his mother relieved her anxiety; and as for his father, the fire was of more consequence than the welfare of a son.

Weeks went by. No one appeared to claim Kate Moran; and only the one woman who had known her mother called at her new home. The child, wanting for nothing, was happy as she could be while her father was in that terrible prison. Her health was fairly established, the injured arm had regained its strength, and she was like a sunbeam in the house of her protector. Very useful she was, too, earning her own living, as her kind friend assured her, and making so many people happy. The anticipation of attending school in the summer sufficed for present enjoyment, and, when Aunt Patsy promised to go to meeting with her some time, she was jubilant. No fear but she would be suitably clothed. Mrs. Richards had a care for that, and by the kindness of this lady the child was supplied with such books as she could understand. Tom Magee saw less of her than he wished, but the thought of his responsibility in regard to her was a strong influence to keep him in the path of duty. Let none of my readers suppose it was easy for him to withstand temptation. The reckless spirit so long indulged sometimes half mastered him, and in hours of despondency the cravings of his appetite were almost irresistible. His perseverance was a wonder, as Wilbur Richards often said when speaking of him.

"Tom has a hard time of it," remarked this friend, after a prolonged interview, in which the former spoke freely of his trials. "I wish he could have a fair chance in the world. He is just beginning to feel his ignorance, and says he must study. His father is a terrible drawback to him in every way. As he gains strength, he grows ugly. If he could get hold of any money, he would find a way to spend it for liquor."

"I hope Tom will be able to control his

own wages," responded Mrs. Richards thoughtfully. "His father can legally claim them, and, should he do so, it would be the hardest thing the young man will have to bear."

"He *won't* bear it," was the reply. "We've talked it over, and that's settled."

Jim Magee, looking forward to the time when he could walk, resolved to assert his authority as a father, take Tom's earnings, and spend them as he pleased. "He'd see if he was going to be ruled by a boy and a woman all his life."

This he said, one morning, as he limped painfully across the floor, then cursed himself, his family, and the doctor. A good breakfast had been prepared for him, but he stood looking from the window, and calculating how soon the snow would disappear. Suddenly he turned, and with a fearful oath swore he would have some liquor. "I'll go to Murphy's if it kills me. I don't want nothing to eat. I've been in hell all winter; now I'll find something to cool my tongue."

Seizing hat and crutches, he left the house, and, if his strength had been equal to his will, he would have walked rapidly. As it was, however, he moved slowly, and hardly had he started when Patsy Quinn saw him. Divining his purpose, and charging Kate to admit no one during her absence, she made haste to inform Tom that his father was on the road. "Look out, now!" she added, with a shake of her head.

"I will," was the reply. "Just wait till I see Mr. Riley; I shall want you."

Mr. Riley understood the matter at once, and not only paid to his assistant what was then due, but also advanced a day's wages, every cent of which was placed in the hands of Patsy Quinn, who was again at home before the lame man had reached her house. She hated the very sight of Jim Magee, and despised him heartily; yet she waited to speak with him.

"Good-morning," she said pleasantly. "I didn't expect to see you out so soon; thought you'd wait till the snow was gone. We'll likely have good walking before long."

"Yes," answered the tired man, resting upon his crutches. "I couldn't stay shut up no longer, though it's tough work for me to walk. That devil of a doctor made a crooked leg for me."

"That *drunken* doctor, you mean," rejoined Patsy. "Strange you should trust a drunkard when you know so much about them! Won't you come in and rest awhile? I had to go out, this morning, but I left the coffee-pot on the stove. A cup of coffee always seems to do me good. Come in, and have some; you'll get home the better for it."

Magee was indignant; yet, withal, so tired, it seemed impossible for him to take another step. Without saying a word, he passed through the door which was opened for him. "It's a good while since you've been to Lion's Mouth before," remarked his hostess, nothing daunted by his sullen looks. "You've had a hard siege of it. I don't know nothing how you'd got along, if you hadn't had such a good boy. Tom's improved wonderful! working early and late to keep you and his mother. Set right up to the table, and have some coffee. I thought, one spell, you'd die; and I hain't a doubt but what you would, if Tom hadn't made you so comfortable. He's got his name up for being the smartest lad this side the river. Don't drink a drop, and works steady as an old man. He made up his mind to it; and, when he makes up his mind, folks may know it means something. I shouldn't wonder if he turned out a rich man. 'Twouldn't be no stranger than a good many things."

"No; 'most anything happens," answered the hitherto silent man. "Tom's well enough in his place. I want to get down to Riley's yard, and find out what kind of a bargain he's made. He ain't quite a man yet, and needs looking after."

"You mean he ain't twenty-one," suggested Mrs. Quinn. "Anybody'd think he was, though, to look at him and see him work. He knows how to take care of himself."

"Where's your boy, Patsy?" This was a cruel question, and therefore was it asked.

"I don't know," answered the unhappy mother, after some hesitation. "Dead, may be; and if he is, I'm some to blame for it. I loved him, but I didn't tell him his duty as I ought to. If I'd read the Bible to him, and told him how God loves us, he might been different. Poor boy! I don't blame him for going off. He couldn't live with his father. The boy had a right to leave a drunken father."

"He'd be thirty years old, if he's living," said the man, than whom none had been more recreant to his duty as a father.

"'Most thirty-two. He's been gone fifteen years, and he was as old as Tom when he went away. I dreamed about him last night—dreamed he come back. I tell you, Jim Magee, it's a dreadful thing to feel you hain't done right by your children! It's bad enough to ruin ourselves, soul and body."

"What's got into you?" now exclaimed the wretched man, pushing back his chair from the table, and regarding his companion with a strangely puzzled look.

"'Tain't whiskey nor the devil!" was the reply. "That's what gets into some people. When you was a young man, you wa'n't so bad as some others; but lately you've acted like one possessed. I wish you'd turn round, now, and be a decent man."

"You can't learn old dogs new tricks," replied Jim Magee, with a malicious grin. "I'm much obleeged for your preaching and your coffee."

From Lion's Mouth, the speaker went to the wood-yard, where he hobbled up to Mr. Riley, and announced his errand.

"Don't owe your boy a cent," was the answer he received. "He takes up his wages as he goes along. He's had quite a family to support, this winter."

"Well, well," said the disappointed man. "For time to come, I'll take what he earns; it belongs to me."

"I guess not, Magee; I made the bargain with Tom, and, as long as he does the work, he's the one to have the pay. Don't try to make a fuss; if you do, you'll get the worst of it. 'Twouldn't be a hard matter for your boy to get clear of you by law. He's made some good friends that won't see him abused."

Tom, coming into the counting-room, said to his father coldly: "You hadn't ought to walked here, this morning. It will put you back more than you've gained for a month. I'm going up the river with the team, and you can ride home."

"I sha'n't ride. When I'm ready to go home, I can go without asking your leave."

Forgetting all prudence, the speaker added: "We'll see who's going to be master."

His next visit was to Murphy's, where, promising to pay for his liquor when Tom's wages were paid, he found no difficulty in procuring all he desired. Before noon, he was so intoxicated that his presence was intolerable even in that vile den; and his son passing the door, the proprietor shouted, "Tom Magee, come and take care of your father! He's drunk, and we can't have him around here in the way."

"Who made him drunk?" asked Tom

"Made himself drunk," was the reply. "'Tain't nothing to me what my customers do, if they only pay up. Heard you said you wouldn't never come into my store again. 'Tain't best to make such promises, if you do feel smart. Guess you'll have to come in now; the old man can't stand no more'n a jumping-jack."

Only the crack of a whip answered this, and Murphy stood staring into the street with dumb surprise. "We'll see," he muttered, and, giving a backward glance to the room where a fierce-looking dog kept guard, started for Riley's wood-yard. There, busily at work, was Tom, who gave no heed to the exclamations of anger lavished upon him.

"Ain't you coming to take the old man out of my way?" was asked at length.

"No, sir, I've something else to do," answered the young man coolly. "I've been paid for a full day's work, and I mean to do it. If you've got into trouble, you'll have to get yourself out, for all of me."

Murphy, excited by liquor, sprang towards Tom Magee, when a well-directed blow felled him to the ground. "Served him right!" was the verdict of the bystanders. Tom's conscience did not trouble him, neither had he any fears of the threatened vengeance; yet, as the hours went by, he thought of his father. Was it his duty to take the drunken man home? He was sorely tried, yet he wished to do right.

Fortunately, he was obliged to pass the house of Mrs. Richards; and, looking up to Wilbur's favorite window, he saw his friend, who beckoned him to stop. "I've been hoping you'd come," was the greeting he received. "There's a family in the basement of the yellow house, poor as can be, and mother wishes to send them a basket of food. The man is such a drunkard that it wouldn't be safe for mother to go. Will you go?"

"Yes, sir, I'll go this evening. I'll do anything to please you, but it's my opinion you'd better get the man out of the way. He hain't no right to drag his family down to hell."

"He can't do that," Wilbur Richards made reply, looking anxiously at his companion.

"Drunkards *have* done it," said Tom, in an excited tone. "Their children, any way, don't have half a chance to get to heaven. You see, they're born ugly, and they can't help it. Then there ain't no chance for the poor things afterwards. I tell you, I *hate* a drunkard anywhere! I don't care whether he wears broadcloth or sheep's-gray, I *hate* him! He's worse than anybody else, except the man that sells him liquor, and they're both too mean to live."

"What is it, my friend? Is there any trouble at home?"

"There must be, by this time," was the reply. "I'm sorry I run on so, but it's the way I think, and I've been dreadfully stirred up, to-day. I want to tell you."

The story was soon told, and the question asked, "What shall I do?"

"Don't you think it would be better to take your father home?" was asked in reply. "I know it is hard, and I pity you, but it seems to me you ought to take him home. You know we hope he will reform. All things are possible with God. Come and see me this evening."

"Yes, sir, I will. I'll need to by that time. And I'll carry the basket."

"WANT SOME HELP, DON'T YOU?"—Page 149.

A little before dark Mr. Riley entered Murphy's rum-shop and enquired for Jim Magee.

"I don't know where he is," growled the proprietor. "I kicked him into the back-room, this forenoon, and hain't seen him since. May be he is in there now."

Mr. Riley looked into the back-room, and there, vainly struggling to rise from the filthy floor, was the object of his search. "Want some help, don't you? Here, take your crutches while I give you a pull. Had a pretty hard bed. Here, Murphy, lend a helping hand. This man can't walk, and, if he's the worse for what's happened to-day, you'll have to answer for it."

Startled by this, the rum-seller gave his assistance, and Jim Magee was lifted into the cart which was to convey him home. Not a word was spoken during the uncomfortable drive. Tom *would* not speak, and his father was suffering too much to make conversation desirable. For once the drunkard was thoroughly mortified. He had accomplished his purpose of obtaining liquor, but he was paying dearly for it. Never was the sight of home more welcome.

His son was obliged to carry him into the house, and it was a work of much difficulty to remove his soiled clothing. In doing this Mrs. Magee assisted, as also in helping him to the bed.

"Do you want anything to eat?" asked Tom, when all this had been done.

"No," was the sharp reply.

"Perhaps you'd like some cold coffee," said his wife timidly.

"Don't want none of your slops," he answered, with an oath.

"Mother, put on your bonnet and shawl, and ride with me as far as Patsy's. I'll come back and look after father. He won't freeze, and this is no place for you. Come," added Tom decidedly. "I'll take care of things."

Mrs. Magee did not hesitate. Trusting her son's judgment, she prepared to accompany him, while her husband kept silence.

The wretched man was left alone. His whole body quivered with pain. His nerves were strung to the highest tension. Each sense was strangely acute, each faculty of his mind unnaturally active.

Memory recalled the days of his childhood, his early manhood, and the later days which had been so darkened by his brutal conduct. Wife and children had been to him only as chattels, subservient to his will. He was to command, they to obey. He had acknowledged no responsibility, no accountability, to One who sitteth in the heavens. The death of his younger children had made no change in his life, except that he had fewer objects upon which to exercise his tyranny.

Tom, fearless Tom, never quailed in his presence. It could not have been fear which prompted the care so lavishly bestowed upon him; and surely the boy could not love him. He remembered the broken accents of prayer to which he had listened. Could it be that Tom was a Christian? Vile and wicked as was this man, he knew there were Christians in the world—men and women who forgave their enemies for Christ's sake. Had he not been an enemy to his son? Had he not doomed every member of his family to ignorance and want?

Baby faces, over which coffin-lids had closed, seemed gazing at him reproachfully, and in very agony of spirit he cried aloud. He *could* not, *would* not, lie there alone, tortured with maddening thoughts and ghostly fancies. Mental suffering so dulled his sense of physical pain that he forgot his weakness until he attempted to rise. Then, falling back upon the pillow, he covered his face, and wept.

CHAPTER IV.

SLOWLY BUT SURELY GOD'S PURPOSES ARE WROUGHT.

IT would be difficult to analyze the feelings of Tom Magee as he sat beside his mother on the rude seat. He did not attempt to do this. For the time he was utterly hopeless. Terribly angry, too, was he; ready to denounce his father in unmeasured terms, yet he kept silence.

"What shall I do?" asked his mother as he helped her from the cart at Patsy's door.

"Stay here till I come back," was his reply. "I'll see then."

"Pretty hard on you, Tom," said Mr. Riley. "I'm sorry for you, but don't get discouraged. The old man won't get out again very soon, if he ever does. 'Twouldn't be strange if he'd finished himself up with Murphy's help. Show yourself a man now, Tom, and don't shirk your duty."

"I don't want to," answered the young man. "But who knows what my duty is? If you do, I wish you'd tell me."

"Well, 'tain't your duty to earn money to buy liquor. 'Tain't your duty, neither, to be knocked round by anybody; but I guess you'd better try and make the old man comfortable as long as he can't help himself. You'll feel better about it if he dies. Don't let him abuse your mother, though. If you've got to choose between them, take care of your mother."

"Yes, sir, I mean to. There ain't much left of her, any way. It don't seem as though she could ever been young."

"She has been, Tom, and she was called a good-looking girl. But she didn't have no chance to be anybody before she was married; and she hain't since. She's always had a drunkard to domineer over her;

first her father, and then her husband." No reply being made to this, Mr. Riley added, "You can go now. There ain't much more to do, to-night."

Tom hurried from the counting-room. At the door of Patsy Quinn's house, his mother waited for him. "Let me go with you," she exclaimed. "I can't stay here. 'Tain't right to leave your father alone. What if he should die? I want to go. I ain't afraid of him. I can pray."

"Then come, mother," her son answered. And the two walked on in silence. "I've got to go to Mis Richards', to-night," he said, as they paused before entering their home. "She wants me to do an errand for her. I don't like to leave you."

"You needn't worry. I told you I shouldn't be afraid, and I sha'n't. I ought to stay here. Patsy says she guesses your father's took his last walk, and you know we want him to go to heaven. He don't know nothing about it, and we've got to tell him."

"Yes," replied Tom absently. "But it all looks dark to me about father. He's awful bad."

"And so was the man you read about last night; but the book says God forgive his sins, and he went to heaven. And the Bible says Christ came to save sinners."

"Yes, mother, there ain't no chance for me if he didn't." Directly the speaker asked, "What can I do for you, father?"

"I don't know. Guess I don't deserve to have anything done," was the reply. "But I'm in dreadful pain. Your mother's here, ain't she?"

"Yes; she came back with me."

"Don't take her off again, Tom. I won't hurt her. I hain't done right, and I'm sorry for it. For God's sake, don't leave me here alone. I'm hot and cold all at once." Then as if ashamed of any relenting, the suffering man cried, "Why don't you do something for me, not stand there glowering, when I'm 'most dead? Likely you want me out of the way, so you can have the house to yourselves?"

At these last words, all the light died out of Tom's face, and all the gladness left his heart. It had been but a little gleam, a little lifting of the load which pressed so heavily upon him; but now the darkness seemed more intense, and the burden more terrible.

Mrs. Magee, who waited in the kitchen, wrung her hands in that pitiful, despairing way which betokens a feeling of utter helplessness. Seldom in her life had she acted from her own choice; always had there been a tyrannical power constraining her; yet her woman's heart lived, and throbbed responsive to each word and act. Her boy was her idol; and now that he had reformed, he was more to her than all things else besides. In the few happy days preceding her marriage, her ignorance had invested James Magee with all manly qualities, and she looked forward with glad anticipations.

If the dream she cherished lacked the fair proportions of many another, it was nevertheless *her dream*, from which she had been cruelly awakened.

"Father, it'll be best to have a fair understanding between us," said the son, in measured tones. "I'm willing to work and take care of you, but you must use a civil tongue. If you'll behave yourself, mother'll stay with you; if you don't, she won't."

"Don't be hard on me, my boy; I hain't done right, but—but—"

Here the speaker broke down utterly, and his wife bent over him with a vague longing to give him strength and comfort. An impatient gesture, however, sent her back to the kitchen, where she prepared supper; and when this was eaten, her son left her.

Patsy Quinn, ever on the alert for news of her neighbors, accosted the young man with her usual eagerness. "How is he?"

"Bad enough," was the reply. "Won't eat

nor drink. But some way, he's different. I had to leave mother to manage him best way she can. He can't abuse her only with his tongue. He's pretty much used up."

"That's a fact, my lad. 'Twouldn't be strange if he's most through. I thought so when I see you going by with him. Your mother told me how weak he is. He ain't fit to die."

"No, nor fit to live neither. I've wished him dead a good many times. I don't now, though. I pitied him to-night. I wish you could go up."

"I can if I take Katy, and she'll like to go. We can come back when the moon's up. I guess I will. Your mother ain't much of a nurse."

At Mrs. Richards's, Tom was sure of receiving sympathy and encouragement. Wilbur was glad to see him, as he was told heartily. "I've been thinking about you every minute since you were here. I wish

I could bear part of your troubles for you."

"I don't," was the quick reply. "You wa'n't made to bear such as I do, though you've helped me more'n anybody knows. Do you remember what kind of a boy I was the first time I come here?"

"I have a good memory," answered the young host. "I thought you the strongest boy I had ever seen."

"And the wickedest?"

"No; I discovered that you had a generous heart."

"Everybody has, perhaps, if folks could find it."

"Then I hope you'll find one belonging to Mr. Patten. Do you know him?"

"I've seen him. He used to live the other side."

"Yes, he's only been this side a few weeks. The daughter, whose wages paid the rent, was taken sick, and they were obliged to move."

"What's the matter with the girl?"

"People think she has consumption. The woman who washes for us told mother, and she said the family don't have enough to eat. Patten has been on a spree now for about six weeks."

Up to this time, not a question had been asked regarding matters in Tom Magee's home; but before he started on his errand of mercy all was told.

"There is hope," exclaimed the listener joyfully. "Only do your duty, and trust God for the rest. He is able and willing to save. Christ made an atonement for the sins of the whole world; and whosoever cometh to him, even at the last hour, he will in no wise cast out. O Tom! how much good you can do with your strength and your influence. You ought to be singing thanksgivings every day. I heard about your helping the old lame man, that lives up on the hill. He thinks you're the best boy in the country. He says the tracts you gave him were worth more to his soul than the bread and meat was to his body."

"But you see I don't deserve the credit for that. I promised to do good for you, and that's your work I'm doing. I always think what you'd do, and try to do my best."

"And your best is very well, my friend. Mother says, too, that you must have given me some of your strength. I am feeling better this spring, and I think you have been my physician. O Tom! it would almost kill me if I should be disappointed in you. I've set my heart on having you one of the best of Christians. I want you to go to church and Sabbath-school."

"I mean to as soon as I can pay for some new clothes. I promised Jack Wetherbee I'd go with him."

Here Mrs. Richards interrupted the conversation. She had various instructions to give to the almoner of her bounty, and a request to make that he would return and tell her of the sick girl.

Such a place as was this cellar—so dark, so damp, and so dirty! The walls could never be dry; the floors never clean. One large room and two small rooms comprised the tenement, which was seldom occupied. During high water it was not habitable; yet here George Patten had brought his family, and with an oath declared that the accommodations were good enough.

Mary, the oldest daughter, had struggled bravely to do something for her mother and the children; but, at last, the overtasked body refused to obey her will. Of ten children, seven had died, and, dearly as the mother loved them, she could not mourn that God had taken them to himself. But to live without Mary seemed impossible.

"Perhaps father'll do better if I can't work," said the hopeful girl. "Don't give up, mother. They say God knows everything, and it can't be he'll quite forget us!"

Weeks, however, had passed, and yet no help beyond the slight provision made by Mr. Patten, which scarce sufficed to keep his family from actual starvation. At length, one of the poorest of their neighbors visited them, and, seeing their destitution, contributed of her scanty means. Others followed her example, and it was from one of these that Mrs. Richards heard the sad story.

"I'm cold and hungry," sobbed little Willie Patten, as he stood beside his sister's low couch. "Lizzie's hungry, too. Mammie, can't you get well, and buy us something to eat? I'll be good, and never say a single 'nother wicked word if you will."

"I wish I could, darling," was the reply. "Tell Lizzie to come here, and I'll tell you both a story."

"Ain't you cold?" asked the child.

"Not much," answered Mary.

"O dear! I wish I wa'n't. But I be. I'm so cold and hungry I don't care about hearing no stories. Seems as though I could eat all the world up. I wish somebody'd bring a bread big's this house."

Just then, Mrs. Patten hastened to open the door in response to a heavy rap. "Come in," she said, and the young man thus addressed stepped into the room.

"Mis Richards asked me to bring this basket to you," he remarked, as he proceeded to empty it of its contents. "She heard some of you was sick, and thought you'd need something."

Tom was somewhat rude in his manners, and by no means happy in his choice of words, but the poor woman cared not for this. She saw only an angel of mercy; heard only that she was not forsaken.

"I'm thankful to you and her," she said in a choked voice. "We *do* need something. We're badly off."

"This ain't no fit place to live," responded her visitor. "You've got a sick girl, hain't you?"

"Yes; and it's a dreadful place for her, but we can't help ourselves. We're poor."

"There's a drunkard at the beginning of all your trouble!" exclaimed Tom Magee, so moved with anger that he forgot all caution. "You see, I know all about it. I've been through the mill, and I know how to pity you. Mis Richards told me some things she wanted I should tell you, and, if you'll let me sit down a few 'minutes, I'll be glad to. I took my father home from Murphy's just before dark, and I hate rum bad as you can."

Mary Patten heard this burst of indignation, and longed to add her testimony against the accursed stuff. Lizzie and Willie regarded the speaker curiously, their attention being divided between him and the parcels of food spread upon a rickety table. Mrs. Patten moved forward the best chair for her visitor, and then, from a generous loaf, proceeded to cut thick slices of bread, which she gave to her younger children.

"Oh! goody!" exclaimed Willie; while Lizzie, in her shy way, manifested equal delight.

"Guess you knowed somebody was coming, mammie. He's a great, big boy, and there's lots of things on the table. There's a tumbler with something in it, and big bundles, and little bundles; and there's just the biggest bread you ever see!"

"Don't mind me," said Tom, who seemed in no haste to deliver the message entrusted to him. Indeed, he had a purpose in prolonging his stay. He knew that George Patten was in a groggery not far away, where a rough-and-tumble fight was in progress, and thought this family might need some protection should the drunken husband and father come home in furious mood.

"I guess I'll make Mary some tea," remarked Mrs. Patten, as she replenished the fire in a rusty stove. "I didn't know nothing what to do to-night, and I can't tell you how thankful I am you come. If 'twa'n't for Mary, I could bear to live here, perhaps; but she'll die in such a place. She worked in the mill as long as she could stand, and kept up pretty good courage; but now she's all down. She don't see nobody."

"Not them that worked with her?"

"No," was the answer, emphasized with a shake of the head; and then, in a lower tone: "She's ashamed to have anybody know where we live, poor child. I'm ashamed, too; but I 'most forget it when my children are hungry."

"Yes, ma'am," said Tom in a choked voice. "I guess I'll go out, now, and come in bymeby after the basket."

Such eagerness as there was to examine their store of good things the moment the door closed behind him! Even Mary raised her head from the pillow, and took account of their possessions. "You must bring them all in here, and put them in the box," she said. "And, children, don't you tell father."

"I won't tell him a word," replied Willie stoutly. "I guess I know better'n that. He'll take every bit away. if I do." Lizzie also gave her promise, and within half an hour both were sleeping soundly.

A whispered consultation between mother and daughter was soon interrupted by the sound of angry voices from without.

"There's father, and the one that brought the things, and somebody else. They're coming here. O mother! what shall we do?"

"Here's a man that's been fighting, says he belongs here," shouted a rough policeman. "Take him to the lock-up, if you say so. Don't care if he's civil; but we've had fighting enough for once. What say?"

"Shut him up, and be done with it," replied Tom Magee. "That's what I told you to begin with."

"Shut up yourself, and let the woman talk. What say?"

"I don't know," murmured the poor woman, who, despite all his cruelty, clung to her husband with a sort of despairing affection.

The drunkard struggled to release himself from the grasp of those who held him, and, failing in this, uttered a succession of terrible oaths, accompanied with such threats as sealed his doom.

"Help me up the steps with him, Magee, 'Tain't safe to have him round. I can manage him after I get out of this hole. I'll put him where he can't do much mischief to-night."

At this, Mary begged that he might not be taken away. Mrs. Patten, too, joined in the petition, promising to do her best to keep him at home; but they were unheeded, except as they received assurance that he should be at liberty in the morning.

The struggling man was dragged up the broken stairs, and Tom Magee dismissed. The policeman was moving on with his charge, when, by a sudden effort, George Patten regained his liberty, and, rushing forward with uncertain steps, turned into a narrow alley leading to the river. His pursuer followed him slowly, calling upon him to have a care that he did not fall into the water. A dull, heavy splash was the only response.

"Help! help! A man drowning! Help! This way!"

Clouds obscured the moon, and this bank of the river lay in deep shadow. There was the tramping of many feet, hasty orders were given, and for the time one common interest swayed the crowd. The drunkard, who but a half-hour before had been despised by all who knew him, was now an object of deepest solicitude. To save him from drowning, many a man was willing to peril a useful life. But effort was useless, search fruitless; and to the beggared wife and children was told the fate of husband and father.

"Dead! Drowned!" repeated Mary, in a strange, absent way. "How did it happen?" Again she listened, and asked, "Are we to blame?"

"No," answered the policeman. "There wa'n't nobody to blame but himself. If I hadn't 'rested him, he wouldn't run down that alley, but I only done my duty."

This man, by no means devoid of feeling, although it was carefully concealed, thought now to test the sympathy which had been excited. All around him, people were saying that it was well Patten was out of the way. "His family is better off without him. There'll be some chance for them, now he's gone. Poor things! How can they live in that horrid cellar!"

"It's easy to talk," said our policeman. "Words are dirt cheap. How many of you are ready to put your hands in your pockets, and give something to help the family?"

Directly there was an exploration of pockets, and one remarked: "Move them out of that hole to-night. There's two vacant chambers in the house where I live, and I'll pay a month's rent." This proposition also met a hearty response; and before ten o'clock, Mrs. Patten was established in some large, airy rooms, with plenty of food for days to come.

It had all passed so quickly that the great change was hardly realized. Some poor rumseller would miss one of his customers, and there would be one missing from the number of those who polluted the air with their foulness and profanity.

Tom Magee worked, that evening, saying little, but thinking much. When all was done, he went to Mrs. Richards and reported what had transpired, then turned towards his home. Here he found Patsy Quinn, who still watched with his mother. They were troubled by Tom's long absence, and shocked when told the reason of this.

"If Patten hadn't any soul, 'twould be a good thing he's dead," said the young man. "He didn't do nobody any good here, but it's dreadful to think where his soul is now."

"Don't, Tom! Don't talk about it," exclaimed Mrs. Magee; and her husband would have joined in this cry, had he not with iron will controlled himself. He asked no question, but he heard every word which was spoken. He knew when Patsy went away, knew that Tom carried a sleeping child from the house, and counted the minutes while the boy was away.

The next day and the next passed with no appearance of amendment in the health of Jim Magee. He refused to have a physician, asserting his ability to take care of himself, and yet gradually there came to him the fear that he had nearly finished his earthly course. At midnight, knowing his son to be awake, he said, in a quivering voice:

"Tom, is there any danger of my dying?"

"I think there is," was the reply. "Patsy thinks so, too."

"You wouldn't be sorry to get rid of me. I hain't done you no good, my boy."

"I don't know of any good you've done me," answered Tom honestly.

The man accused himself, yet shrank from this accusation when another repeated it. "I wish I'd done different," he replied. "But it can't be helped, now. It's too late to mend a bad life."

"Tain't too late to do better, father. 'Tain't too late to ask God's forgiveness."

"What do you suppose God cares for such a poor dog as I am? If he knows about me, 'tain't likely he'll be very hard punishing me, Tom. There can't be anything much worse for me than what I feel now."

"There's something better, if you're a mind to take it." And as the young man said this, he felt for his father something akin to affection. "Christ died for you," he added earnestly. "He's ready to forgive you, if you ask him."

"Ask him! I don't know how. I can't."

"Yes, you can, father. Ask him just as you'd ask me to do something for you."

"How do I know he'll hear?"

"The Bible says he will; and every Christian *knows* he will."

"Be you a Christian, Tom?"

"I'm afraid not; but I believe the Bible, and it does me good to pray. I couldn't kept up, this winter, if it hadn't been for that. It's been hard, any way."

"I know it, Tom. I've heard you praying when you thought I was asleep, and you cried."

"Yes, father. I've got enough to cry about, take it all 'round. I've worked hard, but I don't care nothing about that. I'm trying to do somewhere near right, and 'tain't easy. I was brought up to be ugly."

"That means me," groaned the father. "I know all about it. I wouldn't do so, if 'twas to go over again."

"Yes, you would, if you didn't pray, so God would help you do better," replied the son. "Some way, you couldn't help it. You'd drink and swear, bad as ever. You no need to been where you are now.

But then, 'tain't too late to get forgiveness, if you'll ask God."

"You ask him for me, Tom. I'm so bad, I'm afraid to. You ask first, and then, perhaps, I'll try."

As there had been a struggle in the mind of the elder man, before making this request, there was also a struggle in the mind of the younger before complying. It was not easy for him to kneel in the presence of his father, but he did so; and as he assumed the attitude of prayer, every feeling of resentment died out of his heart.

"O God! forgive my sins, for Christ's sake."

This was all the father could say; and this was sobbed rather than spoken.

There was little sleep in the house that night. Mrs. Magee, roused by the sound of voices, came from the chamber, and through the slowly passing hours listened, with half-suppressed breath, to the confessions of her husband. Not to her were these confessions made; indeed, he seemed unconscious of her presence, although her name was often upon his lips. The fear of death and the accusations of an awakened conscience tortured him into an acknowledgment of his guilt. He looked to his son for aid and counsel, as one looks to a superior whose wisdom is infallible.

"You'll come home as soon as you can, won't you, my boy?"

"Yes, sir," answered Tom, turning from the door for a parting glance at his father, who thus expressed a desire for his return.

"But likely I'll be hindered some. I'll send a doctor this forenoon, and mother'll take good care of you."

"Yes, she'll do that; but I'll miss you."

"I'm glad you'll miss me," was the hearty response. "Good-morning."

There was some hesitation on the part of the physician called upon to attend Jim Magee. He was pressed with business, and suggested that there were others more at liberty. But Tom was not thus to be dismissed; the fee was tendered, and earnestness prevailed. The doctor was interested; listened patiently to a brief account of the invalid's sickness and symptoms, and promised to make an early call.

This day, the first hours of which had brought to our young friend such surprise, had been selected by his old companions as that which should witness his entire discomfiture. Their plans had been carefully arranged, and they were sure of success. They were not to be defied.

Under a dilapidated fish-house, on the banks of the river, were found various stolen articles; and in the same place were also found some tools, such as are used for forcing locks and opening windows. These last were marked with the name of Tom Magee, and the rudely engraved figure of an owl.

Mr. Riley was first notified of this discovery during Tom's absence, and stoutly maintained the young man's innocence of any participation in the robbery with which he was charged, remarking, "The goods were stolen only a month ago."

"Four weeks ago last night," was the response.

"And Tom has worked for me steady all winter. I tell you he don't know anying about that scrape."

"He don't work for you nights?"

"No, and he don't steal, neither. I'll warrant he can tell where he was that night, and prove it. The gang he used to be with hate him, and mean to make trouble for him. You'd better overhaul them, not come round here, trying to make a fuss with a boy that's trying to do as well as he can. I tell you I'd trust him anywhere. He could steal from me, if he wanted to steal from anybody."

"How do you know but what he does?"

"How do I know! How do I know anything? I watched him a month all the time, and I calculate I found out what he was up to by that time. He used to be one of the hardest boys, either side the river; but I'd go bail for him now anywhere, and I'm good for five thousand." As this was said, the speaker slapped his hand upon a well-filled pocket-book; and, the wood-cart being driven into the yard, he shouted, "Come here, Tom. Here's a man wants to know where you was four weeks ago last night."

A flush of anger overspread Tom's face, then the hot blood receded, leaving him ghostly pale, yet he manifested no fear. He bowed coldly to the officer, who regarded him with severe scrutiny, asking, "Can you give an account of yourself for that night? If you can, I want to hear it."

"Yes, sir." Tom took from his pocket a diary, and, turning to the date in question, read, "Went home at dark. Found mother reading in my new Bible. After supper, come down the river, and stopped a few minutes at Patsy Quinn's. Then went to Mrs. Richards', and stayed till ten o'clock. Went home, and read five chapters in the Bible. Then went to bed."

"That's your story. What Mrs. Richards is it where you staid till ten o'clock?"

"Mrs. Richards at the head of Third Street. Wilbur Richards' mother."

"And you visit there, do you?"

"I go there."

"Well, 'tain't for me to say but your story's true. But what about the cellar under the old fish-house? I suppose you know there's one there."

"Yes, sir. I helped dig it, and stone it."

"Thought likely. Some of your property's been found there, and some of Perley's. How do you account for that?"

"They couldn't got there without hands."

"Your hands?"

"*No, sir!*" This denial was thundered out in a startling tone.

"Hold on, Tom," exclaimed Mr. Riley.

"Don't get mad. Shouldn't blame you, but 'twon't pay. I know you've told the truth, and I'll stand by you through thick and thin. You ain't obliged to tell about the tools. You ain't in court."

Some further conversation followed, which resulted in a visit to the city, where the wood-dealer made good his word in regard to bail. It was not likely to prove a very serious matter, after all; but Tom felt it keenly. Remembering Jack Wetherbee's warning, he knew to whom he was indebted for this annoyance. He went about his work as usual, but towards night he grew despondent. Clouds were gathering, and the way seemed dark before him. There was so much in his past life he wished to forget, that the thought of having it recalled almost overwhelmed him. He was "only a lad," as Patsy Quinn often said, when speaking of him.

"Always darkest just before day," said his employer. "Hold up your head, and tell the truth, and you'll do well enough. I'll stand by you, and there's enough knows how you've done, this winter. Ask Wilbur Richards if he remembers your being to his house that night, and ask Patsy if she see you when you was going home. Face the whole thing like a man. We all know you've had a hard row to hoe, but keep up good courage! There can't nobody make me believe that any of the city boys broke into Perley's store. What do you think about it?"

"If the boys did it, they had a leader outside. I know some things about it, and, if worst comes to worst, I'll tell what I know. There's always enough to put up boys to do bad, and one bad one always wants a dozen to keep him company. I know, because I've been in that box. If the good folks would only be as busy as the bad ones, they'd do something. Some of them are, and they're like angels in the world. There's Wilbur Richards; if I was good as he is, I'd be satisfied."

"He *is* good, no mistake," said Mr. Riley. "His mother's one of a thousand, too. Money don't set them up above other folks. Better go over and see them, and see what they say about this scrape."

The advice was heeded, and, without unnecessary delay, Tom explained the reason of his coming. Wilbur Richards referred to his journal, in which was a note of the visit made four weeks before, and an outline of the conversation which occupied their time. He read from this for the encouragement of his friend:

"'Prayed together before separating; and I believe the Spirit of God is moving upon the heart of the young man. If I may be the means of leading him to Christ, I shall not have lived in vain. He is a noble-looking fellow, and I am more and more attracted to him—' I don't know as I ought to have read the last line," said Wilbur, with a smile. "I don't wish to flatter you, so that you will think of yourself more highly than you ought to think."

"I'm not likely to think a great deal of myself just now," was the reply. "I wish I could change my name, and forget the old one."

"Make the name honorable and honored. That's part of your work in the world, and there is plenty more waiting for you. Mother visited Mrs. Patten to-day, and she told how kind you had been. Mary said she shouldn't know you, you've changed so much. Come, Tom, cheer up! Be sure God remembers you, so there's no need of being cast down. Tell me of your father."

There was much to tell; and both speaker and listener were so interested that the passage of time was unnoted. "I don't think father'll live long," said Tom at length.

"Possibly not," was the reply; "but I have faith that he will die a Christian. I'd like to see him; but you are the one to help him, Tom. I'm thankful you prayed with him. Your mother, too, how is she?"

"Patient, and trying to do as well as she

can. Poor woman! She's been ordered round so all her life she don't know how to manage for herself very well; but she's learning. You wouldn't know our old hut for the same place 'twas six months ago. When the curtains are down in the evening, and there's a good fire, it's almost pleasant."

The striking of a clock reminded the speaker that he would be expected at home, and, with a heart somewhat lightened, he bade his friend good-evening. At Lion's Mouth he found Rob Morrison and Jack Wetherbee waiting for him—the former looking anxious, the latter hopeful.

"How are you?" cried Tom heartily.

"How are *you?*" was the response.

"First-rate! Never better." And a cordial shaking of hands testified to the pleasure of this meeting. "Got into trouble, Rob?"

"Not much; but there's trouble for somebody."

"So I've heard; and I've got track of some of my tools. Where's the new bird?"

"Gone. Packed off the night Perley's store was robbed, and that's the last of him."

"Where was you?"

"Over to Jack's. Staid all night."

"And the others?"

"Round town in different places. They didn't go near Perley's. He couldn't get one of them there. Fact is, we've all missed you, Tom, and your preaching that last night ain't forgot. I've wished I'd swore off when you did."

"Then do it now! It's time; and there ain't nothing smart in tossing off a glass of liquor as though 'twas cold water. Any fool can do that."

"I know that. If a fellow could go to the captain's with plenty of money, and just call for what he wanted, there'd be some fun in it; but I'm tired of the dirty old nest. It's getting awful slow there."

"And you think 'twould be better at Captain Blood's?" said Tom enquiringly.

"Yes; don't you?" was the reply.

"There's more lights there, and likely the cards are cleaner. Shouldn't wonder, too, if they have cleaner tumblers to drink out of, and their drink costs more. But, if they're being made into drunkards, what's the difference? They'll all go to the same place in the end; and there ain't a meaner rumseller in the city than Captain Blood. 'Twa'n't only last week a woman asked him not to sell her boy any more liquor, and he laughed at her for getting excited about nothing. That boy's just as certain to be a drunkard as he is to keep on going to the Captain's. He's over twenty-one, and can spend his money as he's a mind to. If I had a million dollars, I wouldn't spend a cent of it in that saloon!"

"Come, Rob," said Jack, looking to his companion to divulge the object of this interview.

"Yes," was the reply. And Rob proceeded to offer his services in clearing Tom

Magee from all suspicion of being connected with the robbery. "I know all about the tools, and I'll tell, if you want me to. Perhaps 'twill make trouble for the rest of us, but I'm bound to see you cleared. A bad promise better be broke than kept. If it hadn't been for you, I'd gone under, last summer."

"And if it hadn't been for me, perhaps you wouldn't made so many bad promises. Boys, what a devil I've been, and gloried in it! Let me clear *you*, Rob. You're in more danger than I am. You hain't swore off from the cursed drink, and I have. Come, join Jack and I; we're on the right track."

"I'll see," was the reply. "Jack's been preaching to me like a minister, and I promised to go to Sabbath-school when you do. I'll be a bully scholar, won't I? I don't know hardly how the Bible looks; but my old grandmother knows it from beginning to end. She'll be in kingdom come to have me study it."

"And you'll go to meeting and Sabbath-school any time I do?" remarked Tom.

"Yes, siree; just when you say."

"Then we'll go next Sunday. It's Friday, so we'll need to be making our plans for it."

Rob Morrison looked somewhat disconcerted at this turn of affairs. He had not counted on such ready acceptance of his proposal. "You've caught me this time," he said at length, with a forced laugh. "You caught me napping."

"Why? Didn't you mean what you said?" asked Tom.

"Yes, I suppose so," was the reply; "but I didn't think you would take me up so quick."

"But I have, Rob. I wa'n't thinking to go so soon myself; but it's always best to strike when the iron is hot. I calculated on a new suit of clothes before I went, but 'twon't make much difference. We can go once without a lesson, can't we, Jack?"

"Yes," answered the boy, who had been an attentive listener to the conversation between his friends. It was a matter of surprise to him that Tom was not more anxious in regard to the affair which had so excited Rob and himself. This surprise he expressed, adding, "I thought you'd feel dreadfully."

"So I did a while; but I'm getting over it. I've got a clear conscience about that stealing, and I guess I can stand the rest, though I'm ashamed enough of having belonged to 'The Owls.' You'd better leave them, Rob."

"Guess I shall have to, if I go to meeting and Sabbath-school. Can't get along with all three, and I don't want to. Your leaving, and the new bird's row, about done for us."

"Good for so much!" exclaimed Tom. "I'm much obliged for your offer; but I hope I sha'n't need your help. I don't want to get the boys into a scrape. I've done enough of that. I'll meet you on the bridge Sunday morning at ten o'clock, and we'll find a chance to finish our talk some other time. Good-night."

"Tom, my boy, is that you?" asked Jim Magee, as he heard a firm step in the kitchen.

"Yes, sir, it's me," was the reply.

"I thought you never'd come. It's been a dreadful long day. Your mother's read to me, and took good care of me; a good deal better than I deserve. But I wanted you."

"The doctor come, father?"

"Yes, and he's going to try and patch me up, though he says I am pretty much worn out. You're a good boy, Tom, to look out so for me; working hard to feed me, when I hain't been no kind of a father to you. I'm glad you've come."

Mrs. Magee did not say she was glad to see her son; but her face lighted up with a joy which could not be simulated. "He hain't spoke cross but once to-day, and then he was sorry," she murmured as Tom was standing by her side. "I can't bear to think of his dying. The doctor says the chances are against him. "He'll be a cripple, any way, if he lives."

Supper was eaten, and, after the sick man's wants had been supplied, it was time to think of rest.

"Tom, couldn't you read a chapter, and pray, while your mother's here? I want you to, and I guess she does. I can't pray myself; I'm so wicked, 'tain't no use trying. Tom, my boy, don't you never drink another drop of liquor as long as you live. I don't mean to. If I get well, I'll see if I can't fight the devil that's in me, so he'll have to give up on the liquor business. It's hard to lay here; but I'm to blame for it. There ain't nobody else to blame except the drunken doctor. Curses on him! Come, my boy, read something good, so I sha'n't want to swear. I'm so used to the bad words, they keep coming into my mind, and the more I try to forget, the more I can't."

Without hesitation, Tom took his Bible, and commenced to read. This soothed his own feelings, and the prayer he offered seemed to bring down a blessing. His mother was more hopeful, his father more subdued; and as for himself, he had gained new strength and courage. They lay down to sleep with the consciousness that God's protecting care was over them, and awoke in the morning refreshed. Even the father, under the influence of a powerful sedative, slept quietly.

Of course Patsy Quinn had heard of the discovery under the old fish-house, and was impatient to know how it affected her neighbor. She expected to see him the previous evening; but, having been disappointed, she waited anxiously for his appearance in the morning. A few words satisfied her. Tom was all right. She remembered seeing him pass her house soon after ten o'clock the night of the robbery. She would testify to that in court, if necessary. "I went to the door, and looked after you, after I'd seen you through the window in the entry. The light shone out so I could see till you got by the bend. I thought about it next morning, first thing, when I heard what had happened. I knew you didn't have nothing to do with it. I won't keep you no longer, my lad. Good luck to you."

There was a rush to the wood-yard that day. Mr. Riley's business was increasing. Orders were so promptly filled, and Tom was so obliging, that there was seldom an opportunity for fault-finding. "Honesty is the best policy," was the motto of this establishment; and, rough though he was, its owner had the reputation of being an honorable man. As the many customers came and went, he took occasion to commend his assistant, thus forestalling prejudice, and securing friendly consideration for the young man. At night, he gave more tangible proof of his favor by informing Tom that he could afford to pay higher wages. "A quarter more every day, boy, and you ought to save that."

This surely was something for which to be grateful, and the young man's spirits rose accordingly. At home, his mother had occupied herself in making his best suit as presentable as might be, and on Sabbath morning every garment was so scrupulously clean that he had no need to blush for his appearance. His father gazed at him wistfully and proudly, watching him through the window until he was lost from sight.

"There's Mr. Tom coming!" exclaimed little Kate Moran. "Just see, Aunt Patsy, how nice he looks! He's got a white handkerchief with one corner hanging out of his pocket, and his boots are just as black. He's got on gloves, too. His boots ain't wet a bit, so he's stepped real easy. I guess he's going to meeting. Don't you guess so, Aunt Patsy?"

"I don't know," was the reply. "You

can go to the door and ask him. You're as clean as he is."

Tom caught sight of the sweet child's face, and quickened his steps, thus plashing the well-polished boots, much to Katy's regret. As he stopped to speak with her, she praised him a little shyly, asked where he was going, and returned his kiss at parting.

"He *is* going to meeting, Aunt Patsy," she said joyfully. "It won't be many Sundays before we'll go, will it?"

"I guess not, child. When the snow's all gone, and I get a new bonnet, I mean to go. You'll be perfectly happy then."

"Yes, Aunt Patsy, all but about father. You know I can't forget him. I dreamed, last night, that he called me, and said how sorry he was for being wicked. It 'most seems as though he really did say it."

"Well, well, child, don't think about him. You can't do anything for him. You're going to read to me, and I guess we'll go up and see Mis Magee some time to-day. I promised her I would, and the old man asked me the first time."

Time passed quickly, and, when the bells rang for afternoon service, Mrs. Magee welcomed two visitors.

"Patsy Quinn?" called the sick man.

"Yes, Jim. How do you do, to-day?"

"Uneasy and discouraged. Want to swear, and talk as bad as I can, but I won't; though I suppose it's 'most as wicked as though I did. I want Tom to come and read to me."

"I've got a reader here," responded Patsy—"a little girl that lives with me, and she can read 'most as well as Tom. Want her to read to you?"

"Let me see her first," was the reply.

Katy needed some assurance before entering the room where lay Jim Magee, but once there, she looked smilingly into his face, while she waited for him to address her.

"What's your name?" he asked.

"Kate Moran."

"What! Duke Moran's girl?"

"Yes, sir."

"How long have you lived with Patsy Quinn?"

"A good while. All winter."

"And you read to her, you mite of a thing. Let me hear you read, and see what you're good for."

This last was said not unkindly, and, taking from her pocket her own "precious little book," the child began to read. Something in the reader or the story so fixed the man's attention that he forgot all else.

As the last word was read, he brushed a tear from his eye, wondering if God's mercy was sufficient to cover the multitude of his sins.

"Who learnt you to read?" he asked after a long silence.

"Mother," answered the child softly.

"She learnt you how to be good too, didn't she?"

"Yes, sir. She told me about God and heaven."

"You love God?"

"Why, yes, sir. Course I do. Don't you?"

"I don't know, child. Any way, I guess he don't care much about such an old scamp as I be."

"Oh! yes, he does. He loves everybody," said Katy, happy in having an opportunity to reiterate this favorite truth. In reply to further questions, she was able to give a reason for her faith, and during the next half-hour, in her simple way, she preached Christ and him crucified. For all there was of sound outside the room, these two might have been the only inmates of the house; yet there were eager listeners, treasuring every word, and gaining consolation in no limited measure.

Meanwhile, Tom Magee had taken another step in the upward way. Robert Morrison and Jackson Wetherbee were crossing the bridge when he came in sight, both better dressed than himself, yet neither so likely to attract the attention of strangers.

"Didn't know but I'd get a chance to go home," said Rob, with a laugh. "Guess I shall feel like a cat in a strange garret. Had to tell grandmother about it, and she's happy as though she was t'other side of Jordan. She don't go to meeting, but she wants to."

"Then why don't she go?" asked Tom.

"Well, the truth is, she's pretty old, and don't make good work walking unless somebody helps her. The last time she went she fell down, and father told her she'd better stay at home."

"Why don't he go with her?"

"Oh! you wouldn't catch him inside a Gospel shop. Tom, what makes you look so solemn? Anybody'd think you'd been to a funeral."

"I went to a drowning last week, and perhaps I shall go to a funeral this week," was the serious reply. "Who knows? It may be yours."

This effectually silenced Robert Morrison, who was by no means so thoughtless as his manner indicated. For the remainder of their walk, Tom and Jack sustained the conversation, speaking upon various subjects which interested them.

The morning service was enjoyed, and Jack was delighted to introduce two new scholars to his teacher, who guessed at once with whom he had to deal. The class now numbered four, and, judging from the appearance of these four, there would be no diminution of the number.

After school, Jack persuaded his friends to accompany him home, where a frugal lunch was provided. Again they joined the worshipping congregation, and listened reverently to the words of the preacher, who sought to impress his hearers with the necessity of preparing for death.

"We ought to remember that sermon,"

said Tom Magee, as they walked homeward. "We must all die, and we all have souls to be saved or lost. George Patten had a soul. Where do you suppose it went when he died?"

CHAPTER V.

THE DARKEST WAY OFTTIMES SHALL LEAD TO GLORIOUS DAY.

THE transforming power of religion is nowhere more clearly shown than in the lives of those whose feet have touched the lowest depths of vice. Repentant and forgiven, their hearts warmed by a new love, and their sensibilities quickened by communion with the holy and divine, they are indeed born again. If old things have not entirely passed away, those which now appear quite overshadow them. There is ever a looking forward to the grand perfection unto which the sanctified soul shall attain. They have part in the inheritance remaining to the people of God, and, remembering their former low estate, press onward to the prize.

A life of reckless sinning is by no means

a fit preparation for the reception of truth, but the same zeal in good works will yield an abundant harvest. Of this fact, Wilbur Richards had been mindful when he selected Tom Magee as one upon whom to bestow much labor.

Many will pass through the world, mere negative characters, exerting comparatively small influence for good or evil. Not so, however, with our hero. From the very necessities of his nature he must act constantly and decidedly. He must be a leader. His destiny was stamped upon face and figure, rang out in the clear, rich tones of his voice, and echoed from his quick, manly tread.

Long before he dared hope that he was a Christian, those who observed him closely saw the change which some hidden power had wrought. The affair which had so troubled him was settled without injury to his reputation. The real offender was discovered and punished. Through Tom's persistent efforts, the boys disbanded, and were known no longer as disturbers of the peace. Several had been arrested; and thus fear of the law was made to exert a salutary influence.

"Tom Magee's steady to his work as a man. Grows smart-looking every day," said Patsy Quinn, who was scarcely less interested in him than was his mother.

And this mother—how she hoped, and prayed, and smiled, happier than ever before! Rising with the sun, she went about her homely household duties; resting at night with the consciousness of a day well spent. Midsummer's warmth and light pervaded her dwelling. The song of birds filled the air with melody, and wakened a response in her heart. Pausing occasionally in her work, she would stand at the door, and watch the movements of a pale, crippled man, who busied himself in the cultivation of a small patch of land. By some intuition, he seemed to know when she thus watched him, and repaid her thoughtfulness by a friendly nod or a wave of his hand, which was more to her than the fondest words would be to many another woman.

This pale, crippled man, moving slowly and easily fatigued, was Jim Magee, who had so often boasted of his strength. Boasting was not now his habit. Glorying only in the Cross of Christ, his whole life was a struggle towards conformity to the will of him who came into the world to save sinners.

Contrary to all expectation, his sickness had not been unto death. For some wise purpose God had spared him; perhaps to prove the possibility of reform in one who had been thought irreclaimable.

"You'll see old Jim hobbling down here, the first day he gets out," said Murphy, with an oath, when told that his former customer had forsworn liquor. "Tom made him promise when he couldn't help himself. I'll let him have all the liquor he wants, just to spite that cub of his. I've got my back up, and I'll show them what I can do. I've had Patten thrown in my face ever since he tumbled into the river; and the day they found his body, there was a perfect howl round my ears."

All this the rumseller said with an air of bravado, emphasizing his speech with fearful oaths, and looking around defiantly to see who would dare gainsay him.

"Patten's body was the worst sight ever I see," replied an old man, having no fear of the rumseller before his eyes. "There wa'n't nobody round would took care on't but Tom Magee, and 'twas an all-fired tough job for him. I say, Murphy, that boy's a peeler to work, and talk, too. I've got a tract in my pocket he give me, and he made me promise to read it."

"More fool you! He won't come round here with his trash, I'll warrant that. Give me your tract, and I'll light my pipe with it."

"No, siree. That boy helped me home, one night, when you turned me out in the rain; and I won't break my word to him. I'm keeping the little book to read, some Sunday. Hullo! There goes Tom, now; straight as a line, and worth his weight in gold, all because he knew enough to let drink alone. Tell you, 'twas a good thing, after all, when them tools was found. Swanny, his friends turned out thick as bees in swarming time."

To use his own expression, Murphy was "raving mad" to hear this praise of one whom he hated; and, in the strongest possible terms, he asserted his determination to make Jim Magee so drunk he wouldn't know himself.

Weeks came and went, while he waited in vain for Jim's appearance. At length, weary of waiting, and improving what he considered a favorable opportunity, he concealed a flask of whiskey in his pocket, and went up the river.

"Hullo, Jim! How are you to-day? Thought I'd come round and see how you was getting along. Got so you hobble round some, don't you?"

"Yes, I'm a good deal better than I deserve to be," was the reply to this salutation.

"Stay pretty much to home, don't you?" continued the visitor.

"Yes, home's the best place; and I've staid away so much, I want to make up lost time."

"Don't stay too close; we've been expecting you down along. Coming, sometime, ain't you?"

"Guess not. Last time I went down 'most finished me; you remember it, don't you?"

"Well, yes. You took a little too much. Try again, and do better." Here the speaker laughed loudly, reminding Jim of his former ability to outdrink the crowd. When he supposed this flattery to have taken effect, the flask was produced and uncorked. "There, taste of this, and see what you think of it."

Instantly Jim Magee's hand was outstretched. Would he drink, and, drinking, seal his own destruction? His eyes flashed, and great drops of perspiration stood on his forehead. He seized the flask for a moment, held it tightly, and then, with sudden energy, threw it from him. The flask was shivered to atoms, the whiskey saturated the greensward, and the rumseller was livid with rage.

"What did you do that for?" was his first salutation, prefaced with an oath which might have startled the very demons. "That was good whiskey."

"Was it, Murphy? What did you bring it here for?"

"For you to drink. Thought 'twould do you good." It was hard to say this, with the eyes of his companion fixed upon him, seeming to read his very thoughts; but the visitor must make some reply, and maintain some show of friendship.

"You thought, if I drinked that, I'd drink more, and you'd be sure of me. I tell you, Murphy, don't you never bring liquor in my sight again. If I'd drinked it, 'twould been worse than death to me. 'Twould been damnation. I ain't going to lay it up against you; but 'twas a wicked thing to do." The man was confounded, as he listened to these words, spoken in a deep, earnest tone, which was in itself the proof of strong emotion. "Your liquor-selling is the devil's own work, and you'd best give it up."

"I didn't come up here to hear a sermon," was the angry retort.

"And I couldn't preach it, if you did," said Magee. "I ain't fit to preach, but I'm trying to do better than I used to."

"Old fool," muttered the rumseller, as he strode away. "Don't care nothing about the whiskey, but I can't bear to have Jim git the start of me."

"That was pretty tough," said Jim, hobbling into the house, where sat his wife. "I wanted that whiskey awful, and I can't tell how 'twas I helped drinking it. Did you see?"

"Yes," was the reply. "I trembled for fear, and I asked God to help you."

"Then that was it. I didn't think of God for a minute. I didn't think of anything but just the whiskey. 'Twas the devil tempting me. What would Tom done if I'd drinked it?"

Ah! what would he have done? What would he have said to find his hopes thus blasted? Perhaps a sense of danger oppressed him; for, in the midst of his work he stopped suddenly, and offered a silent petition that God would enable his father to persevere in well-doing. "Give him strength to resist all temptation," was the burden of this prayer; and at night he learned how great had been the need.

"I beat that time, my boy," exclaimed the father.

"'Yet not I, but the grace of God,'" added Tom reverently.

"Yes, yes, that was it; and I'll have all my life to be thankful in. I was mad at Murphy, though, and I wanted to strike him."

"No wonder; he deserves a thrashing."

"You won't thrash him, my boy?"

"No, father. That ain't in my line now." And a hearty laugh testified to the speaker's genial good-nature.

From that time, there was less of fear, mingled with rejoicing, in Jim Magee's home. In his crippled condition, he would not be likely to put himself in the way of temptation; and his old companions carefully avoided his vicinity. Tom's Sabbath-school teacher, and the pastor, who understood how to speak a word in season, were welcome visitors. Everything was so changed that it was difficult to believe what had been; and yet the two upon whom depended this change, were constantly reminded of their past experience. Self-control is not easily learned when appetite and passion have long held sway.

"Up-hill work," remarked Mr. Magee to the clergyman, with whom he was conversing. "I'm afraid sometimes I'll come short."

"Not if you look to God, my friend. The best of us must do that, and the worst of us can do no more. It is God who giveth us the victory through our Lord Jesus Christ."

"Yes, sir, I know that; but it does me good to hear you say it. I'll be through soon, and then I'll see it all."

"You mean, my friend, that your life will not be long?"

"Yes, sir; I don't know how long, but 'twill be short. I had an iron constitution, but it's all broke to pieces. Last winter 'most finished me; but 'twas the best thing ever happened to me. Folks ain't generally thankful for being lame, but I am. I never had so good a home in my life. Wife and I jog round here all day, and at night there's Tom to expect. He always comes good and happy."

"You certainly have reason to be thankful for such a son," said the clergyman.

"Yes, sir, more than anybody knows," was the reply. "And to think he turned round of his own accord, and hain't fell back once. Why, last winter, when I used to hear him pray in the night, when he thought I was asleep, I wanted to scream right out. Every word seemed like a sharp knife in my heart. When he was a little chap, I used to say he was the smartest boy in the country; now I think he's most the best."

Tom Magee's pastor joined heartily in this praise, adding that he hoped the young man would soon make a public profession of religion. Wilbur Richards, cherishing the same hope, had urged the duty upon his friend, who, after some hesitation, said frankly that the time had not yet come. A year's trial must test the reality of conversion.

It did not follow, however, that, because he was not of the church, he labored not *with* it. In his own way, Tom was an earnest worker. Over boys and young men of his own class his influence was unbounded. They would follow where he led; and rarely were they ashamed to acknowledge themselves converts to his preaching. Always ready to help the poor and weak, many a ragged child was happier for having met him in one of his rounds. Lizzie and Willie Patten watched him admiringly, and ran to meet him whenever their mother allowed them to do so. At Lion's Mouth, Katy Moran sat on the doorstep or stood by the window as he passed, waiting for a smile or pleasant word. Some days, when Patsy was at work, she went to Tom's home after school; and such days were holidays to his parents as well as to the child. She would come tripping up the walk, hang her neat sun-bonnet upon the nail appropriated to that purpose, make herself tidy, and then look around for some opportunity to do a kindly act. Never so happy as when allowed to officiate as housekeeper, she would light the fire, lay the table, and prepare supper, all the while talking with animation or humming softly.

Familiar with every plant in the garden, Uncle Jim, as she had been taught to call Mr. Magee, was often informed by her of some new development, and challenged to admire some wonderful growth in leaf or vine. Flowers were her especial admiration, and a stray seed of the English marigold having found lodgment in the soil under the window of her room, she was henceforth rich in floral treasures. Carefully protected and watered, it was as fine a specimen of the old-fashioned flower as one would wish to see. Occasionally, Kate would despoil the plant of some golden crown, that she might admire it in the tiny vase which Mrs. Richards had given her; yet, if opportunity offered, she was sure to bestow the crown upon one of her friends.

One afternoon, she went from school, holding daintily a small bouquet intended for Mrs. Magee. "I'll put one of my own posies with it," she said aloud, as was her way. "That'll pay a little for my new apron Aunt Ann made, and the shoes Mr. Tom bought. He'll like to see the flowers. I know he will. Mother used to say God painted them. O dear! I wonder if father couldn't be like Uncle Jim. Seems as though he might."

Her flowers were greatly praised, and, placed in a conspicuous position, quite adorned the room. She flitted about, moving a chair here, and brushing away a grain of dust there, but looking wistfully at Mr. Magee, from time to time, as though not entirely satisfied.

"What is it?" he asked, at length. "You can't expect a rough, old fellow like me to care as much for posies as you do; but you say all the words, and I'll say amen to them."

"'Twasn't the flowers. I ain't thinking of them," she answered, blushing.

"What then? I ain't very cross, this afternoon, so you needn't be afraid of me."

"I want to say something about my father," she then half whispered. "Aunt Patsy don't like to have me talk about him. But I want to."

"Say on, child, just anything you want to," responded Mr. Magee, drawing her nearer to him, and resting one hand upon her head.

"But I want to ask you something perhaps you won't like."

"Ask anything you want to, and I'll answer the best I know."

"Was my father any worse than you used to be?"

An expression of pain flitted across the man's face; yet he replied promptly: "He wasn't a bit worse in the sight of God."

"I know he took money, and that was what he had to go to prison for; but was he wickeder?" Kate hastened to say.

"No, child; perhaps he wa'n't so wicked.

Rum made him bad, and rum made me bad. But he was the smartest, and it didn't show out the same way. I hain't been an honest man any more than him, and 'tain't likely he's behaved worse than I have."

"Then, couldn't he be good, same as you are now, Uncle Jim?"

"Yes, child, he could be a great deal better than I am. He hain't sinned past being forgiven. 'Twas a thief that the Saviour forgive when he was dying. You've read about that, Katy?"

"Yes," she answered, with a bright smile. "And that's what father is—a thief. I wish I could see father; I'd like to tell him about that, and ask him to pray to God."

"You can pray for him yourself, Katy."

"So I do, Uncle Jim, every day; and I know God hears me, because I feel it in my heart. But it don't seem as though I could wait nine whole years to see father. Perhaps, when I get large, I can earn some money, and go to see him. I know he'd be glad, because he hadn't been drinking that awful stuff."

Jim Magee looked earnestly at the speaker, whose eyes were uplifted to his, wondering how any father could turn from so sweet a child, and feeling a bitter pang of remorse for his own misdoings. It may be that little Kate divined this; for she said presently: " I'm glad you're so good now; and you know God forgives all our sins, if we ask him."

Dear comforter! Truly, a little child was leading the wanderers back to their Father's house, beguiling the way with songs and words of simple wisdom.

Patsy Quinn was a better woman than she had been when she dwelt alone; a far happier woman, too, although she was more serious, and less inclined to idle jesting. Regular in her attendance at church on the Sabbath, she was gaining in self-respect as well as in religious knowledge. Her temporal prospects, too, were improving—

how, she could hardly have told; yet one dollar seemed to do the work of two, and comforts were multiplied. In various ways, she was assisted by friends who were careful not to wound her independence. Kate Moran's support was no tax upon her; indeed, she complained that she was not allowed to do more for the child.

Formerly, she had preferred working in the mill to remaining at home. The din and rattle of machinery distracted her thoughts from herself, and the crowd of faces furnished objects of curiosity. For many long years, Patsy Quinn had wished to forget the past; now, she was willing to stand face to face with her life, and know the full extent of her sinning. To repent and be forgiven was her strongest desire; and yet she craved human sympathy and counsel. Was ever another woman whose experience had been akin to hers—another who, giving so much of blind, passionate love, had been so basely requited? Was there another who had hoped so much only to find each hope crushed by one who had pledged himself to love, honor, and cherish her until death should them part?

She knew there were many disappointed, heart-broken women, but they were not like her—oh! no. She said this often to herself, as she looked around upon others. They had been subdued to meek acquiescence, or conquered to abject servitude; while, in her heart, the anger had burned fiercer for every wrong endured. In assuming the marriage vows, she believed that she gave but measure for measure; and no after-experience could convince her that she had not a right thus to believe.

Conquered! Subdued! Every instinct of her nature revolted against yielding to tyrannical exactions; although she would have shrunk from no sacrifice which love demanded. Too proud to remonstrate, she had suffered in silence—starving, freezing, and yet counting such privations of small moment compared with the hunger of her heart.

If by any possibility of training her husband could have been educated to understand and appreciate her, his habitual drunkenness made it certain that he never would. It is not too much to say that he hated both wife and child: the former, because she refused to work for his support; and the latter, because obedience was refused. Patsy Quinn fostered the defiant spirit of her boy; and, bitter as was her grief when he left her with no farewell word, she rejoiced that he had escaped from his father. Two years longer she dragged out a miserable existence, and then she was free—no one claiming from her aught beyond the common amenities of life. She had drifted away from relatives and friends whom she had now no desire to seek.

Not a tear did she shed over her husband's grave; not a sigh did she give to his memory. Henceforth, she was to live as though he had never crossed her path. This she willed to do, and despised herself that she failed in its performance.

Her son, Holton Quinn, was dead—for aught she knew to the contrary—no message from him having reached her since his departure. Now that she was alone, poor, wretched, and ignorant, she loved him all the more fondly—fainting, starving, for his presence. Denied this, she grew strangely cold and taciturn, until the kindness received during a severe illness moved her torpid heart. Since then, she had been willing to lend a helping hand to any in distress; and Tom Magee's praises of her were not undeserved.

"I love you 'most as much as I did my own mother," said Katy Moran, one evening, when they sat side by side after the day's labor was over.

For answer to this, Patsy kissed the fair brow of her companion, while a tear stole down her cheek. "I wish I was as good a woman as your mother," she said, after a long silence.

"Mother *was* good," replied the child. "She loved God, and tried to do right."

"I guess 'twas easier for her to do right than 'tis for me," was the response. "I'm a dreadful wicked woman."

This same confession Mrs. Quinn afterwards made to Tom Magee as they talked of their personal experience; and, when he answered that she was no worse than others, she shook her head doubtfully.

"I never blamed myself till lately," she said. "I used to think my hard lot was all somebody's else fault; and now I can't see but what a good deal of it was. But I might done different myself. I might try to learn my boy something about the Bible. If I could see him now, I'd go down on my knees, and beg of him to do right. I wonder how he looks, if he's living. Sometimes I wake up in the night, feeling as though he was in trouble. O Tom! I tell you I've done a good deal that I am sorry for: so much, it seems as though God couldn't forgive me."

"Then what do you think of me?" asked Tom. "I've been very wicked; but I believe God has forgiven every one of my sins. And there's father."

"I know, and it just goes to my heart every time I see him. I heard him pray, the other night, and 'twas like he was asking some one right near to him. I wouldn't believed it of Jim Magee, and he drinking so many years. You've done a wonderful work, my lad."

"'Yet not I, but the grace of God.'"

"It's like coming up out of a pit, isn't it, my lad?"

"Yes," was the reply.

"And, Tom, do you care for what you used to? The drink, I mean."

"I don't think about it much now, Patsy, unless I smell it."

"You wouldn't drink wine?"

"No, that I wouldn't, if the King asked me. It's all the same with other liquor for making drunkards; and I'd rather die than be a drunkard. Then there's my promise, I never'll go back on that."

"No, my lad, I know you won't, and you're right not to touch the beer, as they say you don't. You're bringing the boys round wonderful. They talk about you in the mill. Miss Wetherbee says there couldn't anybody changed more than you have. You ain't going to stay at Riley's always, be you?"

"Perhaps not," answered the young man with a smile. "But I'll stay till I'm fit for other work. I'm trying my hand at studying books a little."

"I guess I might been a scholar," said Patsy, resuming the conversation after a long silence. "I could learn anything I tried. But, you see, I was married too young. I ain't quite eighteen years older than my boy."

For once she was inclined to talk of herself; and to no one else could she speak so freely as to this young man. They had many traits of character in sympathy, and many common interests. She taught him some valuable lessons, while he encouraged and aided her. As they were about to separate, she asked him the question which had often trembled upon her lips: "How did you know when you was a Christian?"

Tom hesitated before replying; then, his face radiant with joy, he said, "I knew it by the change in my feelings. My whole heart went out in love to God and Christ. I was willing to do anything or be anything God would have me. I was so happy, I wanted to tell everybody how I felt."

"And did this all come at once?"

"No, I don't think it did; but I can't tell exactly. I kept thinking about God, and praying that he would forgive my sins, and fill my heart with love for him; and all

the time I tried to do what I thought was
my duty. By-and-by, it seemed some way
as though I was forgetting my sins, and
thinking more about God's goodness and
mercy."

"O Tom! that's just the way I feel sometimes. I forget all about myself for a little
while, and then I'm so happy. Seems as
though the whole world was all made over
new."

"That's because your heart's made over
new, Patsy."

"No, no, it can't be that, my lad. There's
my sins all the same, just as black as ever;
and I hain't no right to be so happy.
'Tain't like as though I'd been a good woman
all my life."

"There ain't anybody so good but they
must come to Christ for salvation, just the
same as you and me. That's what the minister says, and the Bible, too. When Christ
was crucified, he made atonement for the
sins of the whole world. So, you see, 'tain't

as though we'd got to do it for ourselves. I think of that when my sins begin to rise up before me like a mountain. Wilbur Richards kept telling that over and over to me, every time I talked about how wicked I'd been."

"Yes, Tom, I know that's true; but I don't seem to get hold of it firm as I want to. May be I will, though, and then—"

"Then you'll be a happy Christian. Good-night."

Patsy Quinn did not care to sleep that night. The blessed truth that she had nothing to do with her sins beyond accepting their full and free forgiveness, with a grateful, loving heart, gradually dawned upon her. She rested in the thought of God's infinite compassion, and, when the morning bells roused her, she did not know whether she had dreamed or waked. She only knew that the burden had gone from her soul, and that a cloud no longer concealed the Sun of Righteousness from her view.

Mrs. Richards, who called upon her

soon after this, was deeply impressed by her glad, cheerful spirit. There was no unwillingness to speak of what God had done for her; no coldness in her manner. So far from this, her visitor felt rebuked by her warm, living faith.

"God has led us by different paths, but I trust we shall both reach the land where there is no more sorrow or disappointment."

"Yes, Mis Richards," Patsy replied to this remark. "I've thought a good many times that the way I've come was darkest of any, but it don't make no difference now. I've got the more to be thankful for, seeing I've more to be forgiven; and I'm sure I never'll be tired thanking God."

The visitor gazed around the homely room, and, contrasting her own lot with that of this woman, wondered that she had ever dared to repine. All unconsciously, Patsy Quinn had preached to her an eloquent sermon. The same afternoon she saw Mr. Magee and his wife; not jubilant as was their friend, yet tranquilly happy, striving in these last days of their married life to make amends for the past.

"I thank you for coming," said the husband. "It's kind in you to think of us. I've often told Ann that we owe everything to you and your son. Tom never comes from your house without being helped, and, when he's helped, we are. He's a good boy to us."

"Yes, Mr. Magee, he *is* a good boy, and I know he must be a great comfort to you. I trust you will live to see him an honorable man. Wilbur expects great things of him, and says Mr. Riley must look for some one to take his place in the wood-yard. Tom is improving rapidly. He must spend a great deal of time in study."

How much no one but himself knew, although his parents were sure that he studied when he should have been sleeping. Thus far, Wilbur Richards had been his teacher, but in the autumn he commenced attending an evening school, where his desire for knowledge received a new impulse. There seemed no limit to his powers of endurance. Working through the day, and studying far into the night, he was never exhausted or overwearied.

Midwinter, however, brought other claims upon his time. His father, whose health had gradually failed through the cold season, was at length prostrated by a fatal disease. Two weeks of watching and assiduous care was all which wife and son could give to him whose hold upon life was fast loosening. Two weeks of suffering such as few are called to endure terminated the earthly career of James Magee.

There was hope in his death. Nay, more, a full assurance that he had entered into the rest which remaineth for the people of God. Yet the penalty of his sin followed him to his dying hour. He should have lived to a good old age, each day marked by some noble act, and some advance in the upward way. He *might* have done so much. He *had* done so little. This was his constant regret.

"Tom, my boy, try and do good enough to make up for me," he once said to his son. "Don't let our name be cursed. I've helped pull down a good many. I tried to count, the other day, but I couldn't. You'll help folks up, my boy."

"I mean to," was the reply. "Our name sha'n't be cursed. I mean to make it honorable."

The first honor was awarded to this name when it was registered in the church-book, and Tom Magee was acknowledged as "a member in good and regular standing." A year's trial had proved his sincerity, and his strength to resist temptation.

Never came a happier day to Wilbur Richards than when this friend publicly pledged himself to a life of holiness. Not alone did he stand in the presence of the great congregation. Others were by his side making the same vows. Among these were Jackson Wetherbee and Robert Morrison; the latter having been led step by step, until at last he acknowledged allegiance to the Heavenly Master.

"I never'd done it but for you, Tom," he exclaimed, as the two talked together. "God bless you, and make every day of your life better than the one before it! Grandmother thinks you're near perfect, and father's given up laughing about religion since you talked to him. He don't try to discourage me, either."

Mr. Morrison was too wise to do that; for, ridicule religion as he might, he knew that his boy needed its restraining influence. His mother's prayers and counsels had been unheeded. Deeply she had grieved, but now a brighter day had dawned upon her. She witnessed the solemn service which gave to the church so much of youthful vigor and enthusiasm, gazing with tear-dimmed eyes upon the scene over which angels rejoiced.

She did not see the man who, coming in

late, took an obscure seat, wishing to be unobserved. She did not know that the cherished hope of years gave some promise of fulfilment. Not until she was leaving the house, and her arm was drawn within that of her son, was she aware of his presence. "Thank God!" she then ejaculated fervently. "Thank God!" she repeated again and again, with closed lips.

Robert walked by her side in silence. Later, when he entered her room, he said, "We'll keep on praying, grandmother."

"Yes, child," she answered, laying her hand upon his head as he threw himself at her feet. "My faith's greatly strengthened. Many a time I've sat here Sundays, thinking over about your father, and wishing he was a Christian, so to train his children right; but I never thought about your teaching him till lately. God's ways ain't like ours, and he knows best. Blessed be his name, he don't need to ask us about it. You've got a great responsibility on you now, Robert. All the family will be looking to you to see how you live."

"I know it, and I mean to do as well as I can. But I've got a good deal to fight against. I'm quick-tempered, and it don't take much to make me flash up, before I think. The bad words are almost out before I know they're coming; and then I feel so guilty, I'm almost afraid to pray."

Didn't the good old grandmother know all about this? Hadn't she watched him, anxiously noting the flushed face and parted lips when some opposition or disappointment troubled him? "You ain't so hasty as you was a spell ago," she said, in her homely way. "Since you give up liquor and tobacco, you've been a different boy."

"I guess I have," was the hearty response. "I was growing ugly every day, and I knew it. I don't know what I'd come to if I'd kept on. I've done so many things I'm ashamed of. When Tom Magee left us, I was one that swore he should come back, and drink just as he used to. I didn't believe he'd hold out; though, way down in my heart, I almost hoped he would. Isn't he *splendid*, now, grandmother?"

"He's good, and that's the best praise. He's going to make a smart man. I suppose he'd been smart anyway, if he'd kept on drinking. Folks called his father smart."

"Yes, and Mr. Magee was good at last," said Robert musingly.

"Yes, at last," replied the aged Christian. "He began his work at the eleventh hour; and there's no doubt but he's received his crown. But, child, you'll want some stars in *your* crown; and the souls you help to save will shine as stars."

"Yes, grandmother, I'll want a starry crown."

The speaker was a very child in his simple earnestness that day. His boastful confidence had given place to humility, and his impetuous spirit had been subdued by the grace of God. The change in him was wonderful; less marked than in Tom Magee: yet of such might it well be said, "A miracle has been wrought."

One who had for the first time witnessed the simple rites of admission to a Christian church expressed his admiration for his old companion in characteristic language. "Tom's a stunner," he remarked emphatically. "'Twa'n't no make believe when he promised what the minister read."

"He's pretty much tied up, now," was the reply. "I wouldn't give much for him."

"Yes, you would, Dick. If you was in a tight place, you would rather see Tom Magee coming than a dozen common fellows. Didn't he help you home when you'd got a big brick in your hat, and ain't he always doing something for somebody? The other night, when I went to the prayer-meeting, after Tom give me a lift about that money, the minister read about Christ, as he called him, going about doing good; and I couldn't help thinking Tom was just like him."

"What's he good for, on a time?" was now asked, as though it could never be answered to his credit.

"What do you mean by 'a time?'"

"Why—why—such as we used to have."

"Be you such a fool that you don't know he's got something better to do than smoke a dirty pipe and drink rot-gut whiskey? Don't he study every night, and ain't he going to be a scholar? Ain't he invited to places where you and I wouldn't know what to do with ourselves? He ain't none of your sneaks, though. 'Tain't no matter how ragged and dirty I am; he always comes right up to me and shakes hands, just as though I was good as he is. There sha'n't nobody talk against him when I'm round."

"I wa'n't talking against him," now said the young man who had offended. "I only asked a question."

"And I'll ask you a question. Wouldn't you rather be in Tom Magee's boots than in your own? No shamming. Tell the truth once, if you can, and shame the devil you've served so long."

"I couldn't drink no more liquor."

"Not a drop."

"Nor swear."

"No, siree; nor lie, neither. You'd have to be pious out and out, just as he is. On the square, and no mistake."

"'Tain't all pious folks that's always on the square," was the exclamation which greeted this reply. "Some of them ain't no better'n other folks. They'll make promises, and break their word, same as anybody."

"Well, what if they do! Tom ain't like that. If he told me a thing, I'd know 'twas true anyway. But look here, Dick, you hain't answered my question."

"What if I hain't? I ain't obliged to answer it if I don't want to."

"No; but you ought to be man enough

THE SERMON ON THE RIVER BANK.—Page 245.

to do it. You might as well remember that we've all got to die."

"Hold on there, Robinson, unless you're going to preach a sermon. If you be, take a text, and go at it ship-shape."

By this time, the young men had reached a retired spot on the bank of the river, and disposed themselves comfortably upon the ground. There were eight, all of whom, contrary to their usual custom, had attended church, and all more or less impressed by what they had seen and heard.

"Try your tongue at it, Robinson. Let's see what you're good for in that line."

There was a clamor of voices calling for the sermon; and, at length, Harlan Robinson began to speak, half jestingly and yet half in earnest. Recalling some exhortations which he had heard at different times, he endeavored to repeat them.

"We'll let the text go. 'Tain't much matter about that," he said, by way of introduction. "My friends, we've all got to die, every one of us; and 'tain't right for us to live as though we wa'n't going to die. Every one of us has got a soul, and that's going to live for ever. 'Tain't certain where, but 'twill be in one place or another; and it all depends on how you behave. If you drink liquor, and lie, and steal, you'll go to hell, sure's there is one. No mistake about that. The Bible says so.

"A great many hundred years ago, Christ died on the cross to make an atonement for your sins. If anybody should die to save you from going to State's prison, you'd go down on your knees to him and love him, if you had any heart at all. Now, what's the reason you don't love Christ? Just because you're so wicked. It's a wonder of mercies God let's you live on his earth. You break 'most all his commandments right along; and, to tell the whole truth, you're a miserable set of sinne s."

Here there was some interruption, but the speaker claimed the right to finish his sermon, and proceeded:

"Now, my friends, you ought to repent of your sins, and be good Christians. Then you'd be sure of going to heaven, besides being a good deal better off here in this world. You'd be decent and respectable if you was. You'd give up liquor and tobacco just as Tom Magee has."

"How do you know that?" now exclaimed one of the audience. "There's a sight of men that's Christians that drink liquor, and 'most all of them use tobacco."

"Can't help that," was the response. "Them ain't the kind I mean. It's the best kind I mean, such as Tom Magee, and such as I'd be, if I pretended to be a Christian at all.

"Now, my friends, I warn you all against the dangers of delay. Life is short, and we don't none of us know whose turn 'twill be to die first."

This was more than the careless audience had desired; more, also, than the preacher had intended. Unconsciously, his manner had changed, so that this closing sentence was pronounced in a tone not unworthy its import.

An awkward silence succeeded, broken, at length, by one who exclaimed, "You've done a big thing in the preaching line. Now, couldn't you give us a hymn, and throw in a short prayer?"

Responsive to this, Robinson began to sing a hymn, the refrain of which, "Come to Jesus," is so familiar to all Christians. The voice which lingered over these words was singularly sweet and plaintive, and before the singer had ceased quite a crowd gathered about him.

"Let's have another of the same sort," said a stranger. "That makes me think of the meetings I used to go to when I was a boy."

But Robinson was in no mood to prolong the entertainment, and, without replying to those who continued to urge him, walked rapidly away.

"He ought to prayed," remarked one, looking after him who had left them.

"Shut up, and remember what he said," rejoined another. "There's need enough of it. If Tom Magee was here, he'd tell you so, and he knows. He's got an insurance for t'other side of Jordan, and the rest of us ought to have."

There is still another party whom we must follow on their way from church. This party, consisting of Mrs. Magee and her son, Mrs. Quinn, and Katy Moran, were not inclined to much conversation until they had crossed the bridge and were walking in the river path.

"'Twas beautiful!" then exclaimed the child. "I was so glad, I wanted to cry. Oh! Mr. Tom, I should 'most think you'd want to die, so you could go to heaven right off."

"I hope to go there when I die," replied the young man, smiling down into Katy's upturned face. "But I hope to do some good in the world before then."

"You're doing good every minute," Patsy

responded. "It does me good just to look at you."

Mrs. Magee silently echoed this assertion. Her son was all the world to her; and his presence gladdened her heart as the rays of the sun gladden the waiting earth. She listened while her companions talked of what had transpired that day.

"Do you feel any different?" asked Mrs. Quinn hesitatingly, not quite sure that Tom would consider this a proper question.

"I feel as though the name was written in my forehead," he replied. "It seems as though the whole world knew that I have promised to live soberly, righteously, and godly. 'Twas just what I've promised a good many times on my knees; but, now I've sealed the promise, I'm happier than I ever was before. Patsy, you and mother must join the church; and don't put it off very long."

"Give me a year, my lad, same as you wanted. Then, if I hold out—"

"Hold out! You can't go back."

"No, no! I don't mean that," the woman hastened to say. "But I want to feel a little surer of myself."

Time passed, and, judging by her works, Patsy Quinn was growing in grace, laying aside many habits which had been so long indulged that they seemed a part of her very nature. She was gentle and tender, forgiving and humble. She, to whom so much had been forgiven, could not justly refuse to pardon those who had offended against her. If only her boy would return, her cup of blessing would overflow.

In some measure, Tom Magee supplied his place; and when, by an arrangement advantageous to all concerned, two families were united under the old roof, she rejoiced that her life of loneliness was at an end. Mr. Riley, having purchased the house at Lion's Mouth, wished Tom to take a lease of the premises. Repairs and additions were to be made, giving ample accommodations for four people of simple tastes. An acre of land was enclosed, and through the winter various plans were discussed for cultivating this land. Spring opened early, as if to give our friends an opportunity to test their plans before the first enthusiasm had subsided. All shared in the work of arranging beds, planting, sowing, and weeding. Flowers and vegetables were intermingled. A rustic arbor, the pride of the household, was covered with scarlet runners, from the brilliant blossoms of which humming-birds sipped their dainty food.

Every square foot of the garden boasted some peculiar treasure. But for her ideas of duty, Katy Moran would have spent every waking hour in admiring birds and flowers. As it was, she gave double diligence to her tasks, that she might gain time for her favorite recreation.

To this there was but one drawback. Her pet kitten, beginning to develop a cat's propensities, lay in wait for the bright creatures whose songs made the air vocal with their music. Flitting from the neighboring treetops to some broad leaf or mound of earth in search of food, many an ill-fated bird fell a victim to puss's remorseless appetite.

"I can't love you, if you kill the darling birds," Katy exclaimed, one day, while examining the variously colored feathers she had found under an old currant-bush. "I must ask Mr. Tom to carry you off where you can't never come back."

"But you'll miss your kitty," said her friend, when she made this request.

"I know it," she replied, in a choked voice. "But I'd rather have the birds, if I can't have but one. My Sabbath-school teacher says, sometimes we have to decide between two ways, and then we must think about it a good while, and make up our minds real strong. Then, she says, we can't have everything, and so we must choose what we want most. I want kitty, and I want the birds; but I can't have both. Will you take kitty away, Mr. Tom?"

"Yes, Katy, I'll take her, and thank you for the lesson you've taught me."

"What lesson?" she asked wonderingly.

"The lesson of choice," he replied. "If there was something you *ought* to do, and something entirely different you *wanted* to do, which would you choose?"

"I'd do what I ought to, because that would be right," was her reply.

"But it might be very hard. Do you really believe you could, Katy?"

"Yes, if I *knew* I ought to. But what made you ask me, Mr. Tom?" A look of apprehension overspread her face; and, as her companion seemed not to have heard her question, she repeated it.

"I was thinking," he said, at length.

"Was you thinking of my father?"

"Yes, Katy, I was."

"I'll be grown up when he comes out of prison," she half whispered. "Perhaps he'll want me to live with him. If he does, I must. Don't you suppose he'll be a good man some time?"

CHAPTER VI.

THE TEMPTER AND THE TEMPTED MUST EACH HIS BURDENS BEAR.

TOM MAGEE had seen Duke Moran a sullen, unyielding man, whom punishment had not conquered, and who gave no token of repentance. Never a tear, never a quivering lip or softened glance betrayed emotion.

"He works like a machine," was the description given of him by the officer having him in charge. "He hain't disobeyed orders since he come here, but I count him one of our hardest cases. He hain't complained of sickness, though he's fallen to the floor twice in a dead faint, and I often caution him against overwork. The chaplain has tried to gain his confidence, but it's of no use."

It may have cost Duke Moran an effort to maintain the indifference with which he met his visitor, but, if so, the effort was well concealed. He listened to what the young man said without asking a question. Once only his face flushed as his daughter's name was spoken. He did not so much as raise his eyes to his companion.

"Have you any message to send her?" asked Tom.

"No," was the laconic reply.

"But if she knows I have seen you—"

"She needn't know it," interrupted her father. "Better keep it to yourself."

"Perhaps so," responded the young man. "Perhaps it would have been better if I had not come; but, now that I am here, I have something to tell you which I hope you will remember. There are six people pledged to pray for you every day while you live: Mrs. Richards and Wilbur, Mrs. Quinn and Katy, my mother and myself. We have been praying for you for more than a year, and some time you can calculate about how many prayers have been offered. Good-by."

The prisoner was human, and, brutalized though he had been by the long and excessive use of alcoholic drinks, it must needs be that something of humanity remained. Yet he would not allow one glimpse of this to be seen. Back to his work he went; this break in prison life producing no visible effect.

Tom Magee was sadly disappointed in the result of this visit. He had hoped to find the bad man's heart softened; hoped, also, to have some comforting word for Katy, who was beginning to feel deeply the disgrace which attached to her.

After giving to Wilbur Richards a detailed account of his visit, he said: "Now, what shall we do?"

"Pray," was the reply. "Praying breath was never spent in vain. You and I know that by experience. It will not be best to tell Katy that you have seen her father. Seven years more of confinement may work a marvellous change in him. And then, if he should claim his daughter, she will be old enough to decide for herself. She will be a young lady, a very lovely one, too, if we can judge from present appearances. I hope she won't be spoiled with flattery."

"I don't believe it is possible to spoil her," answered Tom warmly. "She's a sincere Christian, if there ever was one. She understands things, too, better than a good many grown people, and flattery won't amount to much with her. Of course she'll know she's handsome. She can't help it."

"No more than you can help being aware of the same fact in regard to yourself," said Wilbur Richards, smiling at the earnestness of his friend. "There, now, don't blush like a girl, but thank God for giving you such a passport to favor. It is better to attract than repel, and your work is to win souls for heaven."

Thus was the young man beguiled from his despondency, and presently he was engaged in an animated discussion of ways and means for benefiting some poor children in the neighborhood.

Patsy Quinn knew of his visit to the prison, and regretted that no apparent good had been accomplished; yet, remembering her own past obduracy, she was not discouraged.

"You're not sure Duke Moran will ever be any better than he is now?" said Tom, in reply to some cheerful remark.

"No, I ain't," she made answer. "We ain't sure anybody will; but then, you see, Duke's got feelings same as other folks, and 'tain't noways likely but what your going to see him made him think. He couldn't help thinking about you after you come away. You told him how you happened to take Katy?"

"I told him all I know about it—just what anybody could see. It's all strange to me now. That was the turning point with me. If I had left her and kept on fighting, I might be where Duke is."

"Yes, you might, my lad, and the rest of us not been much better off. I don't allow Katy to talk about her father, but I know she hain't forgot him. She told me, the other day, she wanted to earn a lot of money before she's eighteen. That will be when her father gets out. Mis Richards wants to pay everything for her. She'd take her right home, and be glad to."

"Does Katy want to go?"

"Not unless we want to have her. For my part, I don't see how we could get along without her. Seems as though I should give right up, if she went off."

Just then the child came bounding in, radiant and happy. No wonder she was the joy of the household; its pride and inspiration. If her father had seen her, he might not have been able to resist her influence.

Wretched man! He was not so insensible

as he seemed. Had he once looked in the face of Tom Magee, his stoicism would have given way. How he longed for night, and the solitude of his cell! He finished his allotted task, scarcely knowing how, and took his place in the rank of silent men, whose faces he had never seen. His brain was confused, his heart throbbed wildly.

Alone, in the darkness, he thought of his wife and child. He remembered how he had sworn to love and cherish her who had braved the anger of friends that she might give herself to him. He had loved her, as such as he may love. He recalled the time when her lightest word thrilled his inmost soul; when he would have laid down his life for her. Having some generous impulses and noble characteristics, her presence stimulated these into the semblance of true generosity and nobility; while she, believing his passionate declarations of undying love, consented to become his wife.

He was a skilful workman, and might

easily have acquired a fortune. But he could not serve two masters. Men of his temperament must choose between total abstinence and drunkenness. Men of his nature will become brutes, under the influence of intoxicating liquor. His wife, too proud to return to her friends, clung to him through all abuse and poverty, dying while he lay drunk by her side. Often since his incarceration Duke Moran had wondered if his child was living, and sometimes he had longed to see her.

Did he look forward to the time when he would be free—free to stand once more in the blessed sunshine, outside a prison's walls? Rarely. Ten years seemed an eternity to him. He expected to serve his full term. How could he tell what might be then? His very name might be forgotten.

The night after Tom Magee's visit he felt a wild longing to know something of the world from which his visitor had come. He had wished to be alone that he might think; before morning dawned, he desired nothing so much as to escape from the companionship of his own thoughts.

The next day, his abilities were tried in a new department of labor, requiring more of skill and judgment. He welcomed this change, grasping eagerly the more delicate tools. He was obliged to think more of his work, and thus the hours were somewhat beguiled of their weariness, but there was an undercurrent of thought he could not quite ignore.

Six people praying for him! He could recall the faces of every one. Mrs. Richards and her son—he had seen them many a time, and knew well how luxurious was their home. He would have liked to be the owner of such a home. In his way, he had been ambitious, and a half sigh escaped him as he remembered his lost opportunities.

From time to time, his work was examined, and he knew that it was satisfactory.

The next day, a model was placed before him, which he was to imitate. He studied it, seeing where it might be improved, but doing simply what was required of him. Was he a mere machine? Was he content with the round of prison labor and prison discipline?

"It can't be but what the leaven's working in his heart," said Patsy Quinn, months after Tom Magee's visit. "Folks can fight against God and conscience a good while; but he don't have drink to help him, and he'll have to give up some time. You must go to see him again. If it wa'n't wicked, I'd hope he'd never'd come out of there. Just as sure as he does, Katy'll think she ought to go and live with him; and it don't seem as though I could bear that. Could you, Tom?"

"I don't know," replied the young man. "I don't allow myself to think of it. I don't know as we're doing quite right to keep her here anyway. Mrs. Richards could bring her up differently from what we can. Wilbur says she has a great deal of musical talent, which ought to be cultivated. He could teach her music. She is twelve years old now."

"Yes, and old for her years. She understands some things now better than I did when I was married. She wants to learn how to do all kinds of work. She asked me yesterday how long 'twould be before she could earn money."

"She thinks too much about earning money," said Tom, a little impatiently. "I'm able to support her and mother."

"Yes, my lad, I guess you be. Folks say you'll get any price you ask, pretty soon. You're mighty quick at figures, and what's more, you're to be trusted. Riley says it's a pity you shouldn't do nothing but head-work; but he's glad they wanted you in the counting-room. He says, though, you won't stay there long. There's a good many got their eye on you. I'm that proud of you, my lad!"

"Patsy, do you remember the night I took Katy home?"

"Yes, Tom."

"So do I. God's hand has led me all the way since then; and I have nothing which I did not receive from him."

The position now occupied by the young man was not of his own seeking. When asked to enter as clerk the counting-room of the largest corporation in the city, he had been far more surprised than were his friends. It was *what* Mr. Riley expected, and what some others *knew* would occur. He could go back to his old employment, if he so desired; but it was absolutely certain that he never would do this.

At twenty his future was assured, and Wilbur Richards was proud of having helped him in the upwardway. The friendship of these young men was beautiful to behold. Each was influenced by the other; unconsciously often, yet always for good. Both were earnest workers in the vineyard of the Lord; both striving to live at their best, and both looking forward to the recompense of reward.

"I have so much work of my own now, and you are getting so strong, you can afford to release me from my engagement to work for you," Tom remarked smilingly, as they were discussing some new plan for Christian labor. "Where you need muscle for a hard pull, call on me, but you can do your own talking. Your powers of persuasion have been fully tested; and I've no intention of taking the words from your mouth. I'll be a teacher in your school, but you must be your own superintendent."

"I can't do nearly so well as you, Tom, in such a place," was the reply. "I believe I feel as much as you; but I don't impress others as you do. Why, you dear fellow, I almost envy you, though I wouldn't take from you one jot of your power. It's a glorious thing to live in this world, even if one can't do everything."

Tom smiled, looked around the room in which they were seated, then, gazing into the face of his companion, extended his hand to grasp one which had so often been outstretched to him. "I am a wonder to myself," he said after a short silence. "God's goodness to me is new every morning, and fresh every evening. If I could find fitting words to express my appreciation of his mercy, I am sure I could move some hearts to love him."

"You do win some to love him, my friend. You seem to me to be always finding opportunities to do good."

"I don't find them, they find me," was the reply. "But one can do so little, and there is so much to be done. It's a wonder that Christians are not more active, and I hope I sha'n't be considered uncharitable if I say it's a wonder they're not more friendly. It's of no use trying to do good to a poor man or woman, when you're determined to keep them at arm's length.

And children are more sensitive about such things than grown people. Every coarse, rough boy has a certain amount of vanity, and brags about being as good as anybody, though he knows all the time that he's a poor, miserable fellow. Christians ought to understand that, and act accordingly."

"There is one who does," Wilbur Richards made reply.

"Yes, yourself," responded Tom quickly. "I remember the first time I came into this room, and the first words you ever spoke to me. I felt as though you were as far above me as the heavens are above the earth, but you didn't seem to feel it."

"Tom, you're a king in your way. I saw what was in you that day, and now, thank God, others are beginning to see. Everything goes on well at home?"

"Yes, we never have any trouble there. Mother and Patsy are about as happy as two women can be, each in her own way, and Katy has but one trouble. I wish I didn't feel sometimes that I ought to give up Kate to your mother, but I couldn't love a sister better than I love that child, and home wouldn't be the same place without her. I can work for her, but your mother is different from mine, and Katy would learn a great many things here that she can't learn at Lion's Mouth, because there's nobody to teach her. She belongs in just such a room as this. I know her place as well as you do. Tell me what I ought to do."

"I can't do that," was answered. "We should be glad to have Katy here, and we would spare no expense in her education; but you have a claim upon her, while we have none. Suppose you leave it with her to decide."

"That would be hardly right. She knows too little of the world to understand how different her life would be, if she should accept your mother's kindness."

"You might explain it to her," said Wilbur Richards, smiling. "To tell the truth, however, my friend, I don't believe she could be persuaded to leave her present home, unless she felt it to be her duty. She loves Aunt Patsy, and Ann, and Mr. Tom, too well for that. You needn't take my word for it. There's a sure way of discovering the truth."

That very evening Katy was consulted, the case being stated as plainly as possible. "Mrs. Richards is a wealthy woman, and will educate you as she would a daughter," said Tom Magee to his protégée. "Wilbur will teach you music, and you will have as beautiful a home as any girl in the city."

The child listened, looking earnestly into the face of her friend. "Do you really mean that you want me to go away?" she asked, at length, in a husky voice.

"I have said nothing about what I wanted," he answered. "That is not the question. Would you rather live with Mrs. Richards than to live here?"

"I'd rather live here than anywhere else in the world," she exclaimed with great spirit. "You know I would. But I don't want to stay, if you don't want me." In her excitement, she had risen from her seat, and was now standing in a half-defiant attitude.

"Come here, Katy," said Tom, extending his hands.

"No," she answered resolutely. "Just tell me if you want me to go away."

"Indeed, I don't want you to go away."

"Then what made you talk so? It seemed almost as it did after father went off, when there wa'n't any place for me."

"Why, Katy!"

She was gone, and the young man was left to his reflections. She was not to be seen again by him that evening; and, despite his explanations and assurances, it was several days before their old relations were re-established.

"I mean to earn money for myself, pretty

soon," she said gaily. "I've planned ever so many things to do with money."

"If I had plenty of money, I'd buy a piano for my little girl," said Patsy. "Then you'd make music for us."

"Yes; and I'd like the piano; but I'd rather live here without it than go anywhere else; and Mrs. Richards says it isn't at all strange that I should. She said I ought to love you better than I do her; and she told me that Mr. Tom would feel real bad if I should go away. Do you think he would, Aunt Patsy?"

"Yes, child, yes. We'd all give up, if you went off and left us. At any rate, I should."

A few weeks after, the woman who had been acquainted with Mrs. Moran when young, and who had never lost sight of her child, called at Lion's Mouth, and asked that Mr. Magee would come to her house, as she wished to see him upon business. This business had reference to Katy. A bachelor uncle of Mrs. Moran had recently died without leaving a will, and the woman wished Katy to have her share of his property.

"I read Mr. Collins's death in the paper, and I wrote to find out about it. Folks think he's left a good many thousand dollars; but Katy never'll get a cent, unless somebody sees to it. You'll know what to do."

"Yes," answered the young man absently, thinking that now the child's relatives might consider it worth their while to claim her.

Proper measures were taken to establish her title to heirship, and, in due time, notes and securities to the amount of five thousand dollars were placed in the hands of her guardian, Wilbur Richards. By his appointment, made in opposition to the influence of uncles, aunts, and cousins, Katy Moran's rights were secured to her beyond the possibility of loss. Everything had been arranged with the most solicitous regard for her interests, and henceforth she would be a burden to no one. Her board was to be paid regularly at Lion's Mouth, where she still chose to remain.

She fancied herself rich, and spent the long hours of many a night in considering what use she would make of her property. There was always a thought of her father in his prison-cell; always the home she pictured was shared with him. To save him was the one object of her life; and so strong was her desire for his reform, that, at last, she came to regard it as certain.

Yet a feeling of sadness mingled with the joy with which she anticipated the days to come. There must be a sacrifice on her part. One who had served a term in the State-prison could never be received by her friends. Their home might be far away in some secluded spot where few would care to seek them.

Notwithstanding this, however, she made the most of her opportunities for improvement, studying diligently, and acquiring every fanciful art which came under her observation. One day, surprised by the presence of a piano in the common sitting-room, she clapped her hands, exclaiming, "That's just what I dreamed! Who could be so good? I know, though—it was Mr. Richards!"

It was not Mr. Richards at all, although she was allowed to believe her own assertion. The instrument was hired by Tom Magee, who claimed the right to do this, as also the right to conceal his agency in the matter. Then the days went by, if possible, more pleasantly; while it would have been difficult to determine which of the occupants of the cottage was most engrossed with business. Mrs. Magee was housekeeper, and Patsy Quinn went daily to the mill.

Perhaps Patsy sometimes feared that her friends were drifting away from her. The Magees were not at all what they had been when their poverty was greater than her own, and they were fain to come to her for assistance. Tom was a "rising young man," well dressed, handsome, and affable.

All these things she pondered in her heart, until she shrank from being seen with him as they walked home in the evening stillness. She would hasten or linger that she might be alone. One evening, Tom waited for her on the bridge.

"I thought you would never come," he said a little impatiently. "Didn't you see me?"

"Yes," she answered. "But how did I know that you waited for me? 'Tain't likely you want to walk with such a looking old woman as I am."

"Ain't it?" he asked, smiling. "I know more about that than you do. I've heard to-day that Duke Moran has been sick for a month, and I'm thinking of going to see him. It's three years now since I was there, and the man may have changed. What do you think?"

"Think I'd go," replied Patsy, forgetting herself and her soiled garments. "I've been expecting something was going to happen, and so has your mother. Perhaps Duke will die, and, if he was a Christian, I shouldn't be sorry. His life won't be good for much anyway, and, if he was gone, Katy wouldn't have any more trouble about him. If he's sick, I don't know but you ought to tell her. Perhaps she'll want to go and see him."

"I'll go myself first, and see what kind of a reception she'll be likely to meet," was Tom's reply. "It will be a shame to have such a girl as she is tied to such a man as Duke, even if he is her father. No one could blame her if she never acknowledged him."

"No. But 'twould be pretty hard on him if he wants to do better. I heard her say, once, she wouldn't live with a drunkard anyway, and she means what she says; so Duke won't stand much of a chance with her, unless he turns over a new leaf.

"I'm glad she has decided upon that," said the young man. "I wish every woman would make the same decision. I wonder they don't."

"I wonder, too," rejoined Patsy. "But then, it's easier to wonder than it is to do. Women always keep hoping for better times, and then, if their boys take to drink, they can't turn them off. It wouldn't be right, would it?"

"I don't know as it would, Patsy. If anybody knows just what ought to be done with drunkards, they know more than I do. I'm sure, however, that, if I was a woman, I wouldn't live with a drunken husband. I wouldn't live with a drunken wife, and I wouldn't have lived with my father if he had kept on drinking. I don't believe 'twould have been my duty."

"But you used to drink yourself, Tom?"

"Yes; and, if I had kept on, would it

have helped my case if a dozen others had gone down to perdition with me? Not a bit; and that's why I don't believe in clinging to a drunkard when he's past all hope."

"Who knows when he's past hope? I guess everybody must make up their minds for themselves, and do the best they can; though a drunkard ain't no more likely to reform for having a wife and children to abuse. I've seen enough of the world to know that. But, Tom, there's lots of young men coming on to be nothing but drunkards—some of them, too, that think a good deal of themselves."

"Yes, and there always will be as long as Captain Blood keeps his saloon open. His reading-room is well supplied, and there's always jolly company there; but he is doing more to ruin the young men of the city than all the low groggeries within its limits. Decent fellows won't go to such places as Murphy's, but the Captain's is a fashionable resort."

"Be you acquainted with the Captain, Tom?"

"All I wish to be," was the reply. "He recognizes me as Mr. Magee."

What wonder that a scornful smile overspread the face of the speaker? He had visited Captain Blood the day previous to this conversation, and been favored with a most gracious reception. "Happy to see you, this morning," said the gentlemanly rumseller, bowing low to his visitor. "Take a seat and make yourself at home."

"Thank you, but I'm in haste," answered the young man. "I called to see you upon business, and, if you can give me a few minutes alone—"

"Certainly, certainly," interrupted the host, throwing open the door of a luxuriously furnished room, reserved for his most fastidious customers. "Now, please to be seated, and we will talk of business at our ease."

Tom Magee accepted the proffered chair, and, sweeping back the clustering curls from his forehead, as was his wont, said slowly, "I have called upon you in Mrs. Gay's behalf. She asked me to do so."

The Captain's face flushed, and an angry rejoinder trembled upon his lips. But he was politic. Mr. Magee was rising in the world, and for this reason he kept silence.

"She is very anxious in regard to her son, and wishes you to refuse to sell him any kind of liquor." Still no reply. "Will you comply with her wishes?"

"Really, Mr. Magee, I don't see how I can consistently. I'm always happy to oblige the ladies, but Luke Gay is a man, not a boy in leading-strings. His mother troubles herself unnecessarily. A most excellent woman, but a little overanxious. I have the greatest respect for her and for her son, who, of course, you know to be a fine young man."

So soft, so bland, and yet so hard and cruel! Tom could have borne anything better than this hypocritical sweetness. It angered him, and, as he told Wilbur Richards, it would have been a pleasure to shake the old fellow till his false teeth rattled. But of course our hero did no such thing. Without withdrawing his gaze from the face of his companion, he considered what reply should be made. It came at length:

"Captain Blood, do you know of a more contemptible creature on the face of the earth than a besotted drunkard?"

"Is it your purpose to catechise me, Mr. Magee?" There was just a hint of bitterness in the tone, but the manner was gracious as ever.

"Your remark suggested my question, and it is easily answered," said Tom quietly.

"I have no fellowship with drunkenness; but I don't see what that has to do with the object of your visit."

"It has everything to do with it," was the rejoinder. "Luke Gay is fast becoming a drunkard, and he drinks his liquor in your saloon. Only last night, he was sent home from here in a cab. You know about that better than I do. Mrs. Gay wishes you to prevent this occurring again. Two years ago, Luke bid fair to be a useful man; now, unless some new influence is brought to bear upon him, he will soon go down to a drunkard's grave. He hasn't the constitution to stand what I could. I suppose I might drink liquor forty or fifty years, perhaps sixty, and still have the breath of mere animal life left in me; but Luke can't do this. It would be easy for you to say to him that, to please his mother, you must refuse to sell him any more liquor."

"But the precedent, Mr. Magee! The precedent! I might be overwhelmed with just such requests from women; and if I yield to one, why not to another? I contend that mine is an honorable business, honorably conducted. I keep good liquors, and offer them to the public in a fair, honest way. No one is obliged to buy, and certainly every man ought to know what is best for him. I always regret when a man leaves my place the worse for liquor he has drunk here; but I don't consider myself to blame for it. You must see how I stand. If I keep my establishment, I must sell to those who wish to buy. It's my way of making money."

"Then I must tell Mrs. Gay there is no hope for her son; that as long as he has money, you will take it in exchange for what will ruin him soul and body. That is a plain statement of the case," Tom Magee hastened to add. "If you and I were in the street, I should tell you that your business is one upon which rests the curse of God. Captain Blood, you must know this. How many noble, pure-hearted boys have you seen transformed into vile, loathsome drunkards? There are Justin Moody, and Webster Gates, and Sam Eastman, and Hiram Bowen, and Jay Gerrish. I can remember seeing them come in here many a time when I envied them; but I don't envy them now. It's not often they come here now; but here is where they learned to be drunkards. For all this wickedness laid at your door, put over against it one good deed, Captain Blood. Spare Luke Gay to his mother. You have boys of your own whom you never allow to come into this place. You are wise; but your boys will grow to be men, and somebody else will be making money by selling liquor."

Tom Magee had quite forgotten that he was arraigning the lord of the castle within his castle walls; and, indeed, the lord seemed, for a little, to have forgotten it himself. He knew that his visitor spoke the truth. The five young men whose names had been repeated confronted him at every street-corner. Occasionally, when, "by a run of luck" or the mistaken kindness of friends, they could command a few dollars, they would come in, in the old way, and for one evening fancy themselves gentlemen. But these visits were becoming less frequent, and soon they would cease altogether. A slight movement of his companion roused the lord from his reverie.

"I see we don't think alike about some things, Mr. Magee," he said, in the same tone he had preserved throughout the conversation. "I'm sorry for that; but we won't quarrel about it. You've a right to your opinion, and I have a license for mine. While I keep my saloon open, I must sell to those who come. But I'll have an eye on Luke Gay; and I don't think there'll be necessity for sending him home again in a carriage. Won't you take some refreshment, Mr. Magee? Iced lemonade or hot coffee, sandwich or stew, just as you prefer. We get up such things tolerably, and we'll serve you with the best."

"Thank you, but I've no need of refreshment."

As the Captain bowed his visitor out, six fashionably dressed young men lounged down the steps.

"How's that? A new customer, Captain?"

"Only a business call," was the reply. "Magee understands business."

"And to think where he came from!" remarked one. "Out of the gutter! To my certain knowledge, four tip-top fellows applied for that place in the counting-room; and Magee never thought of asking for it. I don't see how it happened; though he's grand-looking, made up on a large scale, and shapely at that."

Captain Blood was less talkative than usual that morning. Making drunkards! Was that a just description of his business? Honorable was it? So is all crime, and sin, and abomination, under the whole heaven, honorable. Licensed was it? So are the chambers of death, through which one goeth down to hell.

He knew that a large proportion of those who frequented his saloon would become confirmed inebriates. There were some of cool temperament, strong will, and steady nerves, who would settle down into men of average goodness when the cares of life should press upon them. They would not be of the grandest sort, to be sure, but better far than many of their associates. They would drink wine with moderation, stronger liquors when occasion seemed to demand, and so go through the world, suiting their habits to circumstances.

The rumseller understood this. He knew "which was which" as he looked around upon those who came within his influence. He prided himself upon his knowledge of human nature, and seldom erred in his conclusions. He knew that he was amassing a fortune by robbing others of their choicest treasures.

The curse of God! God was not in all his thoughts, but his boys were dear to him as the apple of his eye. He caught his breath with a sigh as he recalled the words of Tom Magee. His boys were children, and—and—a moment after, he greeted Luke Gay with careless ease.

Just here it may be well to follow the career of this young man, for whom a widowed mother wept and prayed. He was her only child; the idol of her heart, and the pride of her life. Not coarse and brutal, with gross tastes and appetites, he shrank from positive drunkenness. But there was a charm in the wine-cup, a fascination in the glitter and sparkle which seemed to surround it, and, ere he dreamed of danger, silken meshes, strong as iron bands, enveloped him.

He was good for nothing in the morning until his system was toned up by stimulants. More miserably weak and wretched than usual, the day following his excessive debauch he was impatient for the accustomed tonic, and lingered for yet another glass after his companions had left the saloon.

"Have a care, Gay," said the Captain, laughing. "Be temperate in all things.

Accidents will happen, but it's best to prevent them when you can."

"Wonder if he's afraid of losing his bill," thought the young man, as he walked towards home. "I must attend to that and some other things, as soon as I get rid of this outrageous headache."

The bill was settled, "other things" received attention, and a considerable sum of money changed hands. Luke Gay's property was fast diminishing. His mother remonstrated, and, startled by the prospect before him, he promised amendment. Tom Magee reasoned, urged, and entreated, quoting himself as an example of what might be done in the way of reform. Captain Blood refused to sell him more liquor. He was getting too low to be tolerated in such a place, and, moreover, he might not be a profitable customer. The unfortunate young man abstained for weeks, then drank until lost to all sense of shame. Again and again were these scenes repeated. When his own resources were entirely exhausted, he appealed to his mother for money, which she refused.

"Never, my son! Never!" she would reply to his entreaties. "All I have I would give to save you; but never shall it go to the rumseller."

A year went by—a year of such trial and degradation as can be known only where strong drink counts its victims. At the end of that time, humiliated by the studied coldness of his former associates, and overwhelmed with mortification, young Gay begged for means to commence business in some Western city. Most solemnly did he pledge himself never to taste of intoxicating liquor, or cross the threshold of an establishment where it was sold. He manifested the utmost sorrow for his past course, and prayed for his mother's forgiveness. Under these circumstances she consented to furnish the funds necessary for his experiment. Friends in Chicago were ready to aid him.

He left his home, and went forth to make a new trial of life.

God only knows how he struggled and how he suffered, how often he was nigh to falling, and yet stood erect. God only knows how he prayed for strength to endure unto the end. He was encouraged by letters from those who thought of him lovingly. Success stimulated ambition, and there was a reasonable prospect that his manhood would triumph.

A few days' illness made necessary the advice of a physician, who prescribed a popular tonic, and went his way, little thinking that he had signed the death-warrant of a human soul. Strength returned, but with it came the old craving for spirituous liquor without the admixture of medicinal drugs.

Like an impetuous torrent long restrained, the terrible appetite swept away all barriers, rushing straight on to endless ruin. Maddened and desperate, what cared Luke Gay for honor or friendship, for promise or pledge? What mattered it, though heaven were lost, if only for a few brief days he might slake his burning thirst?

He drank to unconsciousness, then revived to quaff again the poisoned draught. The weeks were brief indeed to him. He noted not the lapse of time. Suns rose and set, the stars came out and returned again to their secret chambers, but to him all was darkness. Down, down he went, into the very gutters of the great city. Friends sought for him in vain, until he was arrested for drunkenness. Then they cared for him as they would have cared for one whose reason was dethroned. So securely guarded that escape was impossible, they watched over him, waiting for his better nature to regain its sway.

Meanwhile, his mother was informed of his downfall and subsequent prostration. "Bring my boy home," she wrote in reply. "If there is no hope for him, it is better that he come back to me."

He came accompanied by one who for the time controlled him, but, alas! how changed. He had been once a popular young man, now none so poor as to wish for his society. Tom Magee visited him with the hope of effecting some good, and fancied that his efforts were not wholly lost. It had not been an accident which made Mrs. Gay acquainted with this friend, although thus it seemed.

"Must I give up my boy?" asked the mother. "Is reform impossible for him?"

"Not impossible," was the reply. "I will never believe that there is a depth of sin from which one may not with God's help extricate himself, any more than I believe there is a limit to God's power."

Luke Gay did not rebel against his mother's commands to stay within the limits of their home. With his dog at his side, he paced slowly through the garden-walks or basked idly in the sunshine. Occasionally he would start, as if moved by a sudden impulse, and then resume his former attitude.

Little inclined to conversation, one could only guess his thoughts by the varied expressions of his face.

At length, there was a change. He was seriously ill. The family physician was summoned, and his disease yielded to treatment. He had come near to death; lingered, even, at death's door, when his mother asked if something could not be administered which would give him strength.

"I will think of it," was the reply of Dr. Brainard, as he abruptly went from the room. An hour later, he returned with a brother physician. They examined the patient, consulted together, and left without reporting to Mrs. Gay.

She became impatient, and was upon the point of sending for Dr. Brainard when he presented himself.

"Have you come to tell me that my boy must die?" she asked quickly. "It seems to me there must be something which would give him strength."

"There is, Mrs. Gay. Give your son what brandy his stomach will bear, and he will be upon his feet in a week. I am as sure of that as I can be of the effect of any medicine. It is what his system requires."

"And is there nothing else, doctor?"

"I fear not," was the response.

"But, if Luke takes brandy, he will be drunk in the streets as soon as he is able to go out. Some one will let him have liquor."

"Yes, Mrs. Gay, there is little doubt of that. You must decide what is best. I cannot take the responsibility."

"Oh! help me, doctor," she cried. "What would you do if you were in my place? I would rather see my boy in his coffin than see him as I have seen him. Tell me what to do. God pity me! This is more than I can bear. In mercy, take the responsibility upon yourself, doctor, and act as if Luke was your own son."

"I cannot," answered Dr. Brainard. "I don't know a parent's feelings."

"But, doctor, you know—"

"I know I was thankful when my brother was dead. I cannot say more than that. God pity you and help you."

"Try something else for Luke, doctor. The next best thing to brandy. How can I decide! I cannot give my boy what I have implored him on my knees not to drink."

Dr. Brainard exerted his utmost skill to provide a substitute for brandy; but the system of his patient was so poisoned by the use of alcoholic drinks that everything failed.

"I can do no more, and whatever is done must be done soon," he said, as he turned from the sick-room.

Was ever mother's heart so tortured? Was ever mother's love so tried? "O God!" cried this woman in her agony, "how can I let him die!" But what would life be to him? She prayed for wisdom; nay, more, she entreated for some visible token by which she might be guided. She went to the bedside of her son, bent over him, and listened to his short, quick breathing.

"Mother, *dear* mother," he murmured, "I have been such a trouble to you. But now I am going to die. The doctor can't do any more for me. I could tell that by his looks. Don't cry, mother." And he put up his hand feebly to his face. It was with difficulty that he talked; yet he could not be persuaded to spare himself the effort. "I've been your naughty boy, but I have always loved you, mother dear. 'Twas the drink made me bad; and I didn't care for it at first. I went to the Captain's because others did, and because everything seemed so pleasant there. Then, when I got to going down, I couldn't stop. Poor, dear mother, how much trouble I have made you! When I went to Chicago, I meant to make it all up, and I should if it hadn't been for the bitters that doctor prescribed. Yes, mother, I do believe I could have kept on if it hadn't been for that. But, oh! dear mother, I can't ever tell you how that crazed me. And 'twould be just the same again. I know it would if I should try ever so hard. I wish I had died before then. 'Twould have been better for us both, mother, dear mother. I've thought sometimes I might get stronger if—" Here he paused. "Mother, dear mother!"

How he loved to repeat this name, so sweet, so full of tenderness and pathos! All unconsciously he had answered his mother's questionings. The way was plain before her. Never should he reproach her with having held to his lips the intoxicating cup.

"Can you forgive me, dear mother?"

"Yes, my son," she replied. "I forgive you all, and love you as I did when you were my darling little boy. My boy! my baby! Oh! Luke, how much we might have been to each other!"

A spasm of pain contracted the pale brow, a shudder convulsed the weak frame, a quick gasp, and then again the words, "Mother, *dear* mother!"

"Yes, mother knows it all," she said, forcing herself to calmness. "We won't blame each other."

For a few hours, it may be, she held in her own hands the life of her son, and fearful was the struggle through which she passed. Then, when too late, she half-accused herself of his death.

Friends came and went. There were many to offer assistance—some who had been the boon companions of Luke Gay in his better days, and others whose sympathies had been enlisted by his unfortunate career.

Among the latter was Tom Magee, or Mr. Magee, as he was then universally known. He knew the trial to which Mrs. Gay had been subjected; and, although he would not have influenced her in her decision, he felt that she had decided wisely. His presence, always welcome in the sick-room, was doubly welcome here, where was required so much of strength, gentleness, tenderness, and, withal, an intuitive sense of another's needs. It was a rest just to feel the clasp of his hand.

The last night of young Gay's life, he ministered to the necessities of the dying man; striving, also, to inspire the poor, trembling soul with something of his own faith in an Almighty Saviour. "His blood cleanseth from all sin, and he waits to receive you." Over and over was this blessed truth repeated, until the dulled ear heard not, and the glazed eye saw not.

Then somewhere in God's wide domain a human soul, freed from all earthly bonds, took its appointed place. Not you or I, dear reader, may say where was this place. He who sees from the beginning, and knows how strangely blended are our lives, deals justly. One who cannot err, separates "the tangled web of will and fate":

> "He shows what metes and bounds should stand
> Upon the soul's debatable land;
> And between choice and providence,
> Divides the circle of events."

CHAPTER VII.

ALONE WITH GOD, THE GUILTY SOUL DARES OFFER NO EXCUSE FOR SIN.

LET us now return to Patsy Quinn and Tom Magee, as they walked leisurely up the river path to their home. They continued their conversation until they reached the garden-gate, when Patsy said abruptly, "You'll go tomorrow?"

"Yes," answered the young man, looking down into his companion's face. "You are more tired than usual," he added kindly.

"I *am* tired," she replied. "I've been thinking too much lately."

"And working too hard," was the response. "I must see to that."

"Seems to me you see to 'most everything," remarked Patsy, with a warm smile.

"No, I don't," said Tom. "There's one thing I've neglected."

Later, he asked Katy several questions, and made some suggestions, in reply to which she promised to coax Aunt Patsy to stay at home "a whole month." "I've got money enough for us both," said the girl. "I would divide every cent with her. I know she thinks we are all better off than she is; and the other day she told me I should soon get above speaking to such a plain old woman as she is."

"Ah! I see what the matter is," exclaimed Tom, laughing. "The old lady is growing proud. We must contrive to curb her spirit a little."

"Do hear those children," said Mrs. Magee. "What can they find to laugh at so much?"

"O Aunt Patsy! Mr. Tom says you are growing proud. Are you?" asked Katy, coming into the room, where sat the two women, one working while the other rested.

"Proud of what? My hard, brown hands and plain dress?" was the reply. "Folks like me don't have much to be proud of."

There was a root of bitterness in her heart; but the next question claimed attention: "Now, then, aunty, will you just stay at home next month, and not think of the mill?"

"What should I do here, child?"

"Wear your new dress, and look like a lady. Help take care of the garden, and keep me out of mischief. Will you?"

"Of course she will," said Tom. "I will answer for her."

In her present mood, Patsy Quinn did not quite appreciate her blessings. Despite her assertion to the contrary, she was a very proud woman; and sometimes, now that her friends no longer needed pecuniary assistance, she perversely wished that she could go away by herself, and resume her old manner of living. This unhappy mood had escaped the observation of her friends; but, now that their eyes were opened, they would take care that she did not foster such morbid feelings. Tom Magee possessed both the kindness and the tact to put her at her ease, while she would never dream that he had guessed her secret.

The next morning he went early to his business that he might gain time for a visit to Duke Moran. And such a visit! The sick prisoner was overwhelmed with emotion when he announced his name, and the object of his coming.

"I am glad to see you," was the hoarse reply, made after an enforced silence. "I've wanted to see you ever since you were here, three years ago. You've changed since then, I shouldn't known you. I've changed, too."

"Yes, you *have* changed, Mr. Moran. You are not looking as you did when I last saw you."

"No," answered the wretched man; "there ain't much left of old Duke, except the frame, and that's just ready to tumble down. Tell me about my little girl," he added quickly. "She's living, ain't she?"

"Yes, and well."

"Thank God!" These words escaped him involuntarily. "Does she ever talk about me?"

"She hasn't been allowed to talk much about you," was the reply to this question. "But she thinks of you, and loves you."

"Tell me that again," cried the father. "Does Katy love me?"

"Yes, she loves you, and prays for you."

"I remember," said Duke Moran, after a severe fit of coughing, which nearly exhausted his strength. "You told me there was six praying for me?"

"Yes, we've kept on praying all these years."

"There's a good many prayers been said for me. My wife—I ain't fit to speak her name, but she prayed for me."

"And, Mr. Moran, have you never prayed for yourself?"

"I've tried sometimes, but 'tain't no use. I know it just as well as I knów I'm in prison. There ain't but one place for such as I be when they die. The Bible says no drunkard can enter heaven."

"But you are not a drunkard," said Tom cheerfully.

"I was one, and nothing stopped me but being shut up here. 'Twa'n't no good in me that I didn't keep on. I'm just as bad as though I had. You see, I've thought it all over a million times. I hain't thought much else these two years, and it's 'most crazed me. I've wanted somebody to tell it to, though I knew 'twouldn't do any good. I'm glad you've come. Does Kate know?"

"She knows nothing of my coming. She doesn't know that I have ever seen you."

"Does she look like her mother?" asked the prisoner. Then before the question could be answered, he added: "Her mother was a handsome girl, and I promised to love her and take care of her—promised strong as words could promise, and then I killed her. That's the truth," he added, after another paroxysm of coughing. "I'm a murderer, just as much as though I'd cut her throat. I'm glad to say it out loud, I've thought it so many times. It's no use telling me that my sins can be forgiven. Our chaplain says they can, but he don't know about me."

It was a strange scene. This man of stalwart frame, wasted to a mere skeleton, in the conflict with remorse and silence, now so gladly confessing his sins. His large, dark eyes, deep sunken in their sockets, glowed like coals of fire. His bony hands were continually clasping and unclasping. There was no rest for the tortured spirit, none for the poor, worn body. It may be that he did not overestimate when he said that he had thought of this a million times. At first defiantly, scorning the authority of both God and man; then with stoicism, assuming that he could bear his punishment, whatever it might be. But now that it had come upon him, neither defiance nor stoicism availed to shield him from the fierce anger of the Lord.

He had worked until remanded to his cell for rest, and then, proud as he was, begged to be allowed to return to his labor. As his health gradually failed, he concealed his weakness; and it was not until disease had fast hold upon him that his real condition was known. He was kindly treated as one may be whom prison walls enclose; yet this kindness was measured by a strict regard to discipline.

Tom Magee looked at his companion pityingly, his heart so full of compassion that his own words failed him. "Christ died that you might live. He bore your sins in his own body on the tree, and now ever liveth to make intercession for you. God so loved the world that he gave his only-begotten son, that whosoever believeth on him might not perish, but have everlasting life. You believe the Bible?"

"Yes," gasped the prisoner.

"Then you believe that God is able to save to the uttermost all who come unto him through Christ. You are one of his creatures."

"Perhaps I was once, but you don't know about me," was the reply. "I've gone all over my case, and argued it both sides, and there ain't no chance for me. I've broke every one of the ten commandments, from first to last, and I'll have to take the punishment I deserve. I'll be through with this world before a great while, and as for another—" Here the speaker was interrupted by the terrible cough which at intervals convulsed his frame; and when this had ceased, he asked in regard to his child. Listening to a description of her personal appearance and accomplishments, he seemed to forget himself. "She never'd been as she is, if I hadn't been shut up. She ought to be glad I've been out of the way. Little Katy! I wish I was fit to see her, and hold her in my arms, once before I die. How come she to live with you? You didn't use to be very good, and your father wa'n't much better than I was."

"You are right in that, Mr. Moran. Would you like to hear how the world has gone with me the last six years?"

"Yes, I should, if you've time to tell me," was the hasty response to this question.

The young man gave a brief outline of his life since the day he had taken Katy Moran to his home, lingering somewhat over the sickness and death of his father, that the listener might learn how one sinner had gained a hope which failed him not in the trying hour.

"I've drinked a good deal of liquor with Jim, and you say he expected to go to heaven. But he didn't kill his wife, and that makes the difference between us. That's the difference between us, and that's why I can't be forgiven. And you've took care of Katy all this time. I'd thank you for it if 'twould do any good. She'll be grown up pretty soon."

"Yes, Mr. Moran. She is thinking of that, and she calculates to have a pleasant home with her father."

This strangely moved the father. His little Katy proposing to live with him! He had wasted his strength, wasted his life, which was now running to the lees. "I never'll see outside the walls," he said at length. "I sha'n't trouble Katy. There'll be somebody to care for her."

"Yes, Mr. Moran. She has plenty of friends, and she shall never want one while I live."

Warned by the passage of time that he must soon leave, the speaker asked permission to pray; which, being granted, he kneeled reverently, while his companion's burning eyes were fixed upon him. His prayer was addressed to Christ, the Elder Brother, who, having once taken upon himself the seed of Abraham, being made like unto his brethren, being tempted in all points like as we are, is able to succor them that are tempted. Not one thought, or feeling, or wish, or half-defined impulse escapes his omniscient eye. Not one condition or inheritance of evil, or hindrance to right doing, but he knows it altogether.

When Tom Magee knelt, it was as if he entered the presence-chamber of this Man, Christ Jesus; and the faith which inspired his petition waxed stronger as he seemed to see the King in his glory. Lower and lower bowed the head of the prisoner, and deeper grew his breathing, until his lips parted with eagerness. A long sigh echoed the 'amen.'

"And you might been like me?" he said wonderingly.

"Yes, Mr. Moran, I should be a more wicked man than you have been, if I hadn't stopped drinking liquor."

"That's it," exclaimed Duke, with great earnestness. "It's the liquor makes men act so. It's the devil's drink, and since I've come here I've thought 'twas brewed in hell. It's what fills the prisons and the graveyards. Don't you know it? If you do, why don't you preach about it? Tell everybody what a curse it is, and tell them so they'll believe it."

" They *do* believe it *now*," was the reply. "People don't drink it because they think it does them good. Didn't you know it made a brute of you?"

"Yes, and hated myself for it; but any time the first years I was here, I'd drinked it if I'd known I'd go to hell the next minute. There wa'n't an hour when I wa'n't crazy for it."

"And now?"

"I wouldn't touch it. Seems to me I should be a little better if I could hear you pray every day," he remarked, coming back to the subject from which his mind had wandered. "I seemed to feel that prayer, Mr. Magee. It touched a spot in my heart I didn't know was there. Won't you come again to see me? And won't you tell Katy that I love her?" Such a wistful, pleading look as overspread the man's face as he said this would have moved the hardest heart. "Ask her if she won't forgive me, seeing I'm going to die, and, if she'd only write a line to tell me so, 'twould make it easier for me."

The visitor did not trust himself to speak in reply to this, but a purpose which had been gaining strength throughout the interview was definitely settled.

The officers of the prison testified to the uniform good conduct of Duke Moran, giving this testimony in writing. The Governor of the State was a relative of Mrs. Richards, and before the day had closed the first steps had been taken toward obtaining a pardon for this man. He could not long survive under the most favorable circumstances, and surely the ends of justice would not be subverted by allowing him a few days of freedom. Wilbur Richards volunteered to present the matter in its most favorable light to the proper authorities, and there was little doubt that his plea would be successful.

All this was done without the knowledge of Katy Moran, who did not even know of her father's illness. Yet she thought of him anxiously. Perhaps, as some assert, the tie which holds in sympathy those of the same blood cannot be sundered without mutual pain. Certain it is that the young girl decided to see her father. She was fourteen years of age, old enough to decide some questions for herself; and, although she expected opposition, she believed her guardian could be induced to give her consent to the visit.

To her surprise, Mr. Richards assured her that she should see her father within a week, and in response to this she asked so many questions that the whole truth was told.

"Oh! why didn't somebody tell me before?" she exclaimed, when she realized how much there was to tell. "And he's coming out of prison to-morrow!" A new thought intruded upon her. "Where will he go?"

"Ask your Mr. Tom," said her guardian. "He is to manage about that."

"Yes, Katy," answered the same Mr. Tom, when asked if it was really true that her father was to be released. "It is really true; and, if you would like to have him come here, I think we can make room for him. Aunt Patsy and mother think that is the best way, if you would like it."

Katy shook her head thoughtfully, then, after some consideration, said: "I ought to live alone with father. I've always intended to, and, if Mr. Richards will let me spend enough of my money, I should rather do so."

"But, Katy, your father will probably live but a few weeks, and, if you will let me judge for you in this matter, I will try to consider the best good of all."

"You are always right," she replied, sobbing. "But I'm afraid you'll all get tired of father, and—and—"

Tom Magee did not attempt to comfort her in the way which had proved so effectual when she was younger, although he longed to take her in his arms and tell her how gladly he would shield her from all care and trouble. He did, however, express his sympathy for her, and assure her she need have no fear that his patience would be exhausted.

The next morning, she was too much excited to take her accustomed place in the school-room. Watching the preparations made for the reception of her father, she went from room to room, giving little assistance, and scarce able to restrain her tears. It seemed to her that time never passed so slowly, and yet when the hour came for her father's appearance she shrank from meeting him. She had been told that he was an invalid, yet she was wholly unprepared for the change in his appearance. She remembered distinctly how he had looked to her when she last saw him, and could hardly believe it was her father who required the support of two men, as he came, or rather was borne, into the house. She ran to the garden, where she remained until Mrs. Quinn went in search of her

"Come," said the woman kindly. "Your father won't rest till he sees you, and its little enough comfort he'll get this side the grave anyway."

"But, oh! Aunt Patsy, I can't make him seem like father. He ain't as I thought," replied the young girl, clinging to her friend. "I can't make it seem right."

"Have you prayed over it, child?"

"I've tried. But my head aches so, Aunt Patsy. I couldn't sleep last night, and I'm so tired." Here a fresh burst of tears interrupted her words.

Tom Magee came in, and when he said quietly, "I have something to tell you," she repressed her sobs. "I wish to tell you how your father received the announcement of his pardon," he continued.

She was interested at once, forgetting her own feelings as she listened. "And he thought 'twould be better to die there in prison than to come away! He thought nobody would want him outside! Poor, dear father! I'll tell him there is One who wants him and loves him. But you don't know how strange he looks to me," added Katy. "I'll go to him this minute."

"You must teach him how good it is to trust in God's love," said her companion. "You taught me that lesson, and you can teach him."

More the speaker did not trust himself to say, but he touched his lips to her forehead, and she was comforted by this mute expression of sympathy.

Duke Moran was alone when his daughter entered his room. "Father!" This word, breathed rather than spoken, thrilled his whole being. He raised his head from the pillow, and attempted to speak in reply, but only the ominous cough made itself heard. His child was not unlike what he had pictured, except in a certain nameless grace which no language can describe, but which he recognized as she bent over him in her efforts to relieve his suffering. "It won't be long," he said, when he could command his voice, as though he had already acknowledged her presence, and now wished to assure her that he should not long trouble her.

"Father!" Clear and distinct was her voice as she pronounced again the word in which she acknowledged his rightful claim upon her.

"Child! Child! Have you forgiven me? Tell me that, child!" And the restless hands were outstretched to her.

She did not say as might another, "I have nothing to forgive," but, laying her soft white hands in his, she answered, "I *do* forgive you, father; and I want to do you good, every minute of your life."

He raised her hands to his lips, then to his eyes, where they were bathed in tears. Then he withdrew them that he might look again into her face. "Hain't you no hard feelings against me?" he asked.

"No, father," she replied tenderly. "I only love you and pity you, and I'm more glad to have you here than I can tell."

"I don't deserve it, Katy, *my* Katy. I don't deserve anything but the worst a man can get in this world or another. Perhaps you don't know I killed your mother."

"I remember about mother," she said with a sigh. "I know you made her very unhappy, but she prayed for you. She would tell you that she forgives you, and please, father, don't say again that you killed her. It hurts me to hear it, and I want to be happy with you." Truthful, loving Katy! She would not seek to make her father's sin appear less than it was, and yet she wished to comfort him. "Rest, now," she added, as he continued to gaze at her as though longing to speak. "To-morrow we will talk. I am going to stay with you all the time."

"It's too much, my child. It must be you're a Christian. It's only such folks that forgive so much."

"Christ forgives more," Katy made answer. "He forgives all who come to him if they've been ever so wicked. Remember that, father, and please let me go now."

He relinquished her hands, and she went from the room, glad to escape his scrutiny. All the circumstances of her mother's death outlined themselves vividly in her memory, and she knew that her father had not accused himself unjustly. Seeming to feel again all the desolation of that far-off time, she bowed her head upon her hands, and wept with the abandonment of a child. At length, recalling her present blessing, she chided herself for ingratitude, and prayed God to give her a right spirit. She *would* be cheerful, she *must* be cheerful, for the sake of the friends who loved her, and, more than all, for her father's sake. Despite this resolve, however, it was a pale, sad face which was uplifted to Tom Magee as he passed her in the hall.

"She will be happier to-morrow," he said to himself. "She must have time to become accustomed to her father," he said directly after to Mrs. Quinn. "She thought she could go away alone with him, but I knew she would need all the help we can give her."

"Tom, do you expect that man's a Christian?" asked Patsy abruptly, without replying to the remarks of her companion.

"If he is, he has no assurance of it," was the response. "He told me, this morning, that he didn't expect to have his sins forgiven."

"Of course God will forgive him, if he goes to him in the right way. Of course he will," repeated the woman. "When the sinner wants forgiveness, and is willing to take it as a free gift, seems to me the trouble's all over. Duke's been bad enough; but he ain't no worse than a good many others. He killed his wife, but there's women that's had to bear more than she did, and wanted to die when they couldn't. He's been hard punished, if I'm any judge of looks. I shouldn't known him anywhere: and 'tain't strange he didn't seem to Katy like her father. I tell you what, that child will grow old a good many years before he dies. If I hadn't come out of the mill, I should now. She's got to be helped through this, and your mother's got enough to do without taking care of a sick man."

"You're a good woman," was the answer made to these several assertions.

As had been predicted, Katy Moran was happier the next morning. A night's sleep had quite refreshed her, and something of her accustomed cheerfulness returned. Thanks to Aunt Patsy's skill in the preparation of a soothing syrup, Mr. Moran had rested tolerably, and was more comfortable than he had been for several days.

"I don't see what makes you take so much trouble for me," he said to Tom Magee, who assisted him to rise and dress. "You ain't under no obligation to do for me."

"You are mistaken in regard to that," was the reply. "I am under obligation to do all the good I can, and to help everybody who comes in my way. All Christians are under such obligations. That's what we mean when we promise to take Christ for our example, and pledge ourselves to obey his precepts. Of course, you understand that, Mr. Moran?"

"I don't know, Mr. Magee. I never had much to do with Christians, except my wife, till lately; but seems to me they don't all act like that. I knew a wholesale liquor-dealer who professed to be a Christian. What do you think of him?"

The reply which first sprang to Tom's

lips was not spoken. A dealer in intoxicating liquor, whether on a large or small scale, was to him worse than the drunkard, who cannot enter the kingdom of heaven. Such a man, at best, must dishonor the church of which he is a member, and ensure his own eternal condemnation. "I think such a man has strange ideas of duty. He is not such a Christian as I wish to be."

Mr. Moran was quite sure this did not half express his companion's feelings upon the subject; yet he forbore any further remark. He was carefully dressed, and seated in a large arm-chair, when his daughter came in to say "Good-morning," and tell him that he was looking better.

"I *am* better," he replied. "I don't know what Mrs. Quinn gave me for my cough, but 'twas better than all the doctor's stuff."

"Aunt Patsy knows just what sick people need," responded Katy, with a smile. "She is cooking your breakfast now. Will you come out and eat with us?"

"Not to-day, child," he answered. "I shouldn't know how to behave. I've eaten alone so long; and prison fare don't require many dishes."

"Father, please don't say any more about prison. I want to forget about that. We'll think you've been away somewhere, and just come home. Wouldn't you like that best?" In her eagerness, the young girl rested one hand upon her father's shoulder, and looked down into his face to assure herself that he was not displeased.

"I should like anything you do," was his reply. "I'll try and do as you want me to."

In her presence, there was to be no more allusion to the darkest passages of his life. But he would be constantly reminded of them. The contrast between a prison-cell and this pleasant room with vine-draped windows was too great to be ignored. He could not blot out the record which six years of imprisonment had stamped upon his brain. The breakfast, nicely cooked and daintily served, was like nothing which he had tasted for years and years. If his heart did not go out in thanksgivings to God, he was, at least, grateful to those who so generously provided for his comfort.

His daughter was with him most of the day, reading or talking as he desired. She had grown wiser in many things since she sat by the bedside of Jim Magee, and told him of God's love; but the old story was the same in its simplicity and sweetness, neither gaining nor losing through the lapse of time.

"That's all real to you, child," said her father.

"Of course it is," was the reply. "It is just as real to me as it is that you are here, and I am glad to have you."

"Being here seems most like a dream to me, and I don't quite understand how it happened that you come, Katy."

"Why, Mr. Tom brought me first, and

now I stay because it is my home." But for a caution she had received, she would have revealed the fact that she was no longer dependent upon the bounty of her friends.

Patsy Quinn, not wholly trusting Duke Moran even in his weakness, had taken occasion to remind Katy that no good would come from his knowing that she was worth five thousand dollars, adding, "You can tell him some time, if you want to; but now you'd better not say anything about it. We all think so, Mr. Richards and all."

It had required Tom Magee's utmost powers of persuasion to induce Mr. Moran to come home with him; yet he did not allude to Katy's small fortune, from which his support was to be provided. Until within a fortnight of his death, the sick man believed himself indebted to the friends who never wearied of their ministrations. Mrs. Richards and her son were his frequent visitors; never coming empty-handed, and never leaving without having moved his heart to deeper gratitude. During one of these visits, when he had expressed a painful sense of obligation, Wilbur Richards told him that he was under obligations to his daughter, at the same time explaining how it was in her power to meet his expenses.

"And you say she would spend every cent of it for me, if I needed it!" was the father's exclamation. "O Mr. Richards! seems as though that hurt me more than all the rest. I most think sometimes God will forgive my sins after all. He must be better than she is, and she forgives me. I'm glad you told me about it, so I can thank her; but if I was the same I used to be, 'twould be best I shouldn't know it." His intellect was unclouded, and as he would have judged another, so did he judge himself. "I've seen the time when I'd took that money, and spent it for rum. What a wretch I've been! It's best I should die. I might go back, though it don't seem to me I could. You're too good to me; and Tom Magee, seems to me he's 'most perfect. He's taken care of me every night since I came here. Money can't pay him for what he's done; but the Lord can reward him."

When Duke Moran thanked his daughter for her kindness, she answered: "I am glad to do it, father. I'm sure you would do as much for me; and we won't talk about it."

There was now but one subject which interested her, one desire which animated her. That her father might feel at peace with God, and with himself, was her constant, earnest, almost agonizing prayer. He never wearied of the sound of her voice; never tired gazing into the dear face, which grew more beautiful to him with each passing day. With her Bible in her hand, she sat by his bedside, reading passages in which God's love and mercy are clearly expressed; occasionally adding some comment or assurance that no one who comes to God, trusting in the merits of Christ, need doubt of acceptance.

"Dear child," her father would sometimes murmur, forgetful of what she talked, and conscious only of her presence. At length she was permitted to hear him say, "I hope my sins are forgiven. I can't feel sure; but I'm willing to trust myself in God's hands."

To greater confidence than this he never attained. Yet his end was peaceful. After a life of stormy passion and sinful indulgence, his body was laid to rest by that of the wife whose love he had so outraged. His daughter sorrowed for him, although she knew his death had been wisely ordered. Separated though they had been for many years, she had felt sure that he would some time acknowledge her claim upon him. On her part, it had been all giving—love, sympathy, and assistance; while he could give in return only thanks and loving words. Now, the dream and the reality were over. For a few days Katy spent most of the time in the seclusion of her own room, where her friends did not intrude.

"I'm glad to see you brighten up a little," said Mrs. Quinn, as her favorite came to her with a smile. "It's been dreadful lonesome. We've missed you. 'Twa'n't strange you felt bad, child; but 'twon't do any good to mourn for the dead. They're in God's hands, and he'll do right."

That evening some one waited at the gate for Tom Magee; some one who wished to thank him more than any words could express. "I feel it all in my heart; but I can't say it."

"Don't try," was the response. "Just let me see your face brighten again, and I shall be thanked. We have missed our Katy. Lion's Mouth has been a lonely place."

This young girl had felt keenly the disgrace of being a convict's daughter. A whispered remark among her schoolmates had often sent the hot blood rushing to her face. Her beauty, gentleness, and intelligence secured her from positive insult; yet she had often been reminded of her misfortune. Now, death had hallowed this misfortune. She would never again blush at the remembrance of her father. She resumed her place in school, more serious, perhaps, but none the less lovable. Older, in fact, by many years, for the experience through which she had passed, life seemed to her more earnest, and duty more imperative.

It could not be that any one of those who had watched and waited by the dying-bed of Duke Moran could be quite the same as before. Even Tom Magee, conscientious worker as he had been, was stirred by a new impulse. He realized more intensely that souls were perishing around him, that men were degrading their manhood, that women and children were suffering tortures worse than death, while husbands and fathers recked not of the ruin they wrought.

"He's crazy on the liquor question," said one of young Magee's friends. "That is his only fault, and sometimes I'm not sure of that being a fault. He has saved many from ruin already. Now, I never drink a drop of liquor, and calculate to give my influence in favor of total abstinence; but it is a different thing altogether with him. He fights the devil on his own ground, and twenty such men would shut up all the liquor shops in the city, Captain Blood's not excepted."

"I don't quite understand Magee's way of doing things," was the reply to these remarks. "He never makes a fuss. Everything comes easy to him. His strength is unbounded, and his will equal to his strength. Then, his talking is perfectly wonderful. I have attended a good many prayer-meetings just for the sake of hearing him. He is no more ashamed of his religion than he is of his face. I know of a dozen young men he has persuaded to attend church."

"I presume so; and there may be dozens of others you know nothing about. Magee never boasts of his good works. He is what

I call a whole Christian—none of your hypocrites or half-ways, that serve God on the Sabbath, and the devil the rest of the time. He is made up on a different plan. Everybody knows that he will do what he thinks right, and say what he feels to be his duty. Nobody is offended with him, not even Luther Marshall, who is ready to fight any one else who remonstrates with him. Marshall is going down fast. Nothing but his money keeps him up, and that can't last long."

Luther Marshall was one of Captain Blood's customers, tolerated by this gentleman for various reasons, although he had often overstepped the bounds of respectable indulgence. Money kept him up, and the Captain, taking good care that he did not interfere with others, allowed him to come and go at pleasure.

Eight years before, Luther Marshall and Tom Magee were as far removed from each other in position as two boys could well be. But now, the former had acquired a reputation which made him the peer of those who once scorned him. While the good respected him for his upright, Christian character, others admired him for his fine personal appearance, his manliness, and his ability. Gradually, and without effort on his part, he had become acquainted with many young men whose parentage and wealth placed them far above the son of a poor drunkard.

It was not in his nature to count this an honor. Indeed, our hero cared little for antecedents or surroundings; yet, thankful that thus a larger field of usefulness was open to him, he received all advances with cordial good-humor. Between Luther Marshall and himself there were some points of sympathy. The same spirit of independence and impatience of restraint; the same self-reliance and hardihood. True, in one these had developed into positive recklessness; while in the other they but served to give vigor and freedom to every well-considered act. If any one could influence Marshall, this one was Tom Magee.

"Ruining myself, did you say?" asked the young man of his friend.

"Yes," was the reply. "Don't you believe it? No one can drink liquor as you do without being ruined."

"I'm not sure but you are right, Magee; but the fact is, I'm so used to it, it don't seem to hurt me. We get used to anything, and I like a free-and-easy life."

"So yours is free and easy?"

"Well, yes; that's the way I look at it. I don't trouble myself about anything; take the world as it comes, and call it all right."

Though this was said with a show of indifference, the listener was not deceived. He knew that in the breast of his companion there yet lingered some hopes and aspirations which found not their fruition in his present life; and, therefore, he asked: "Would you be willing to sit down alone, and recall all the events of the past week?"

"That's a strange question," was the reply. "I don't believe in recalling. I just push the past behind me, and go ahead."

"But you can't do that, my friend."

"Why can't I, if I choose?"

"Because what has been done in the past makes your life of to-day. The habits of the last year, or of the last ten years, tell upon us fearfully."

"Ten years is a long time to look back. I remember you as you were then."

"I remember myself as I was then," answered Tom Magee. "I was a miserable, dirty, lying, swearing, drinking boy."

"It don't seem to have much to do with you now," was the quick reply.

"But it has much to do with me, Marshall. Nothing but the grace of God changed me; and I need the same grace now to keep me in the right way."

"Do you pretend to say that you couldn't reform when you pleased?" Luther Marshall was interested, and waited eagerly for an answer to this question.

"I *do* say that God's grace has made me what I am. If I was not a Christian, I should be a drunkard."

"You're a tip-top fellow, Magee, bound to go up and make a big thing of living; but it seems to me you could have done it just as well without so much praying."

"I couldn't, Marshall; I am as sure of that as I am that we are talking. Perhaps you don't know how hard it is to give up old habits. It was months and years before I could be surprised in any way without being tempted to swear. As for liquor, I could let that alone as long as my will held firm."

"Of course you could," Luther Marshall hastened to say, without allowing his friend to add a qualifying clause to this last remark. "I could do that myself."

Not long after this conversation, Tom Magee was passing Captain Blood's saloon late one evening, when his steps were arrested by the sound of angry voices. Just then, a young man rushed up the steps.

"Any trouble down there?" was asked.

"Yes; Marshall's crazy drunk, and as full of fight as a tiger. Somebody has made him mad, and the Captain's trying to keep peace. There'll be a row, and I don't want to be mixed up with it."

Magee hesitated a moment, then descended the steps, and without remark went to the room in which he had once spent a most unsatisfactory half-hour. There had been hard drinking. Hard words had been exchanged, and blows were threatened. Captain Blood, mindful of his dignity, endeavored to stay the confusion. The respectability of his establishment was at stake, and he was greatly excited. It would have been easy to call a policeman, but this would have wounded his pride. He caught sight of Tom Magee, and without thought of the concession thus made, said, "I'm glad to see you."

"I came in as Marshall's friend," was the reply. "I will take him home. — Come, Marshall, I am going your way," he added, grasping firmly the young man's arm. "I am in a hurry, and want you to go with me."

"No, you don't." A fearful oath accompanied this denial. "I'm going to kill Sweeny. He insulted me, and no man shall do that and live." He struggled to free himself from the strong hands which held him fast, and, failing to do this, exhausted his vocabulary of profane expletives.

"Clear the room instantly," ordered the Captain, and this command was obeyed.

Only Magee and Marshall remained with the gentlemanly proprietor of this respectable establishment. The rage of the intoxicated man was frightful to witness. He gnashed his teeth, his eyes glared ferociously, and, save that he stood erect, he was like an infuriated beast.

"I can manage him," said his friend, who knew that the Captain's presence was required elsewhere. "Don't fear for me."

A long, weary hour succeeded, during which Luther Marshall was not allowed a moment of inaction. When he ceased his useless struggles, he was compelled to pace the room constantly, his companion encouraging or commanding as occasion required.

"Now, suppose we go home," was said, at length. "The air is getting close, and my head threatens to ache. "How is yours?"

"Feels like a steam saw-mill with forty saws running. Who are you, any way? Seems to me I've seen you before."

"Pretty likely. You saw Tom Magee to-day."

"Oh!" exclaimed Marshall, in a tone of the utmost astonishment, and then suffered himself to be led from the room.

Not another word was spoken until they had walked some distance on the street. Having been kept upon his feet, Marshall was in an entirely different condition from what he would otherwise have been; and, although he required some assistance, he was by no means such a burden to his companion as might be supposed.

"Guess I've been in some queer row, haven't I?" he asked, when he was near home.

"There was some danger of a row," was the reply.

"It was at the Captain's, wasn't it?"

"Yes."

"Well, you're Tom Magee. I've sense enough to know that; but how you came there I don't understand. You don't belong there."

"No, Marshall, I don't. I went there to help you out of a scrape, and I'm glad to see you safe home."

"Well, old fellow, I thank you; and, if I can ever do anything for you, let me know."

"Will you do it, Marshall?"

"Yes, to the half of my kingdom."

"Then abstain from liquor until I see you to-morrow evening, and thus do me the greatest possible favor."

"I *will*, Magee. I'll do it if I live, and I know what I'm saying."

He knew what he was saying, but he did not know to what he pledged himself. Less than twenty-four hours of abstinence could surely be borne, and he had given his word. Thus he reasoned the next morning, when he realized what had transpired.

He had spoken truly when he said that he pushed the past behind him. He gave himself no time for reviewing his life. In fact, he was determined to avoid all serious thinking; and the prospect of spending an entire day away from his boon companions and ordinary places of resort quite appalled him. As for reading, this was simply impossible; and his step-mother and a servant being the only persons in the house, he could not forget his privations in genial society. He would not trust himself to go into the street, lest temptation should prove too strong for him and he forfeit his word. For this reason he confined himself to his room, pleading a severe headache as the reason for so doing.

About noon, there was an interruption— a note from Captain Blood, with a bill for liquors, cigars, oysters, and sardines. The bill first received attention. It was larger than he had supposed, and yet he could not dispute a single charge. Turning from this, he read the note with a lowering brow. The note was brief, courteous, decisive, and full of regrets. Indeed, it was wonderful how so much sorrow could be expressed in such limited space.

Luther Marshall was terribly angry as he realized the full import of this note. The fashionable drinking-saloon of the city was closed to him. He saw himself in a new position. "After all the money I've spent there!" he muttered, with an accompaniment of oaths. That bill should be settled before he slept, though his creditor had begged him to consult his own convenience in the matter. This necessitated a consideration of the state of his finances; and the next hour was devoted to a rigid examination of long-neglected accounts. Figures, which could not lie, forced him to the conviction that he had wasted much of his substance in riotous living. His father had amassed property which he had squandered. This was not a pleasant reflection with which to beguile an idle day.

At dinner, his step-mother observed him closely, but, as she was scrupulously careful never to offend him, she asked no questions. The bill he had received was uppermost in his mind. He had not the money in hand to pay it, and, as I have before said, he dared not trust himself to go out. It was not often he asked a favor of Mrs. Marshall, but now, after some awkward preliminaries, he requested the loan of twenty-five dollars until the next day. The money was counted out to him, and directly the full amount of Captain Blood's bill was enclosed in an envelope properly directed.

The afternoon wore away. Evening shadows lengthened, and he waited for the coming of Tom Magee. He had kept his pledge, but how much longer he could resist the cravings of appetite, and endure the torture of his quivering nerves, was uncertain.

"Well, here I am—what there is left of me," he said to his friend, when they were seated together in his room. "To tell the truth, there is less of me than I thought there was. I haven't ventured outside the gate, to-day, for fear of what might happen. Captain Blood is getting anxious, and has sent me a friendly note. Perhaps you would like to read it. Read it, and tell me what you think of it. It seems to me a remarkable piece of composition. It is short and to the purpose."

"You were surprised at its contents?" remarked the visitor, after reading it.

"Yes, I was. I've known the Captain do a good many mean things, but I didn't expect that. Why, he has made a fortune out of such fellows as I am. You know that."

"Of course I do, and wonder how such fellows will allow themselves to be so duped. I expected the Captain would dismiss you soon. It is according to his way of doing things."

"Well, Magee, tell me about last night. Don't keep anything back. I guess I can stand it, after what I've been through to-day.—There is one thing about it," he remarked, when the story had been told. "I'm glad it was you who came to the rescue, not one of those milk-and-water fellows, who apologize for everything they do. I shall never forget your kindness. Whatever becomes of me, Captain Blood won't be troubled with my company. When my bill is paid, we shall be quits. The money is ready for him, when I can find anybody honest enough to be trusted with it."

"Will you trust it with me, Marshall?"

"I would trust anything, even my soul, with you," was the reply to this question. "But I won't ask you to go to Blood's for me a second time."

"I'll be glad to go for you," responded the visitor. "But I must confess that I'm not quite willing to lose my evening with you."

"I'm not willing you should," said Luther Marshall. "You'll find me here when you come back, and I'll remember that I am your debtor for another kind act. Please count the money," he continued, offering the envelope in which it was enclosed.

The money was counted, and Tom Magee hastened to the saloon, where the proprietor greeted him with some embarrassment, but with no lack of courtesy. Here the money was again counted, the bill receipted, and, without comment from either party, the transaction was closed. One step had been taken towards the reform of Luther Marshall. It remained to be seen whether it was the first of a series, or whether, falling back, he would sink still lower in the abyss of sin. His friend was not oversanguine as to the result, and yet did not wholly despair. Somewhat more than a year before this time, a young lady to whom Marshall was engaged, and whom he loved as well as one may love whose whole nature is debased by the use of alcoholic drinks, forbade him her presence. She did not remonstrate with him in regard to his habits—did not warn him of his danger. Too proud to do this, she had said, "Henceforth we must be strangers." No one could blame her for so doing, yet it had made her lover more reckless. Now, as he sat alone waiting for the return of Tom Magee, he recalled every word, and look, and gesture of Caroline Beard as she pronounced his sentence.

"Well?" he said, looking up as his friend entered.

"Here is your bill receipted," was the reply. "You and the Captain are square, and I hope you will never owe him another cent."

"I never *will*, Magee. I would go to the lowest groggery in the State before I would darken his doors. He is a smooth-tongued villain."

"But there is one thing to be considered, Marshall. No one is obliged to go to his saloon or buy his liquor. It is a matter of choice on the part of his customers. He would soon close up if he had no trade."

"I know that," said Marshall, a little impatiently. "But you know as well as I do, that the Captain throws out all lures and baits. A good many have learned to drink liquor in his saloon, who wouldn't have learned anywhere else."

"I know that," was the reply. "I am not excusing him, but his victims are not wholly guiltless."

"You're a strange fellow, Magee. There is no such thing as getting mad with you, though you have told me some pretty plain truths."

"And have come, this evening, to tell you more, if you will allow me to do so," added the visitor.

"Go ahead, old fellow. Anything is better than my own thoughts, and you can't tell me much I don't know." Seeing that his companion hesitated, Marshall continued: "It's now or never with me. I'm going to the devil without ceremony, or I'm going to cry quits with him for ever."

It would occupy too much space were I to transcribe the long conversation which followed. Tom Magee quite exhausted his stock of argument, entreaty, warning, and remonstrance, appealing to each and every motive which is supposed to influence the conduct of men. As he talked, he prayed; and thus was he answered:

"Bless you, Magee, for what you have done for me. If I am saved, I shall owe it all to you. If I am lost, God will not hold you accountable."

CHAPTER VIII.

JOYS ARE BUT SWEETER FOR THE SORROWS PAST.

FOR two years, the lives of the family at Lion's Mouth were marked with few incidents. Labors, in season and out of season, for the good of others, were so much a matter of course that they came to be considered a part of every day's duties.

Two years more of experience had been given to each of this family, and there was cause for thanksgiving in the result which had been wrought. Mrs. Magee had grown younger in thought and feeling, more intelligent, more cheerful, and more quietly happy. Patsy Quinn looked the same. She never told her age, although the time had gone by when she wished to think of herself as having been always old. As it suited her nature to give rather than receive, it must be confessed that her present position was sometimes irksome.

Tom Magee had made steady progress in all things. He was a better man, because his character was more symmetrically developed. He was wiser in his plans, stronger in his purposes. His salary had been increased, so that he was able to bestow his bounty with a more liberal hand. He was still battling for the right, for God and humanity, making the old name honorable, as he had promised his father he would do. Not "Thomas Magee," but "Tom," as it always had been, and as it should be to the end. "Mr. Tom," Kate Moran called him, although she was quite old enough to lay aside this style of address.

In her advancement, she fully realized the expectation of her friends, being "the dearest, winsomest girl in the world," as Patsy Quinn was wont to say whenever Katy had coaxed her into making some concession. "She won't be turned herself, though. She just makes up her mind, and sticks to it, no matter what happens. Sometimes it seems as though she was just a soft little thing you could twist round your finger; but you'll find out the contrary of that, if you give her a chance to show it. Folks don't talk much about old Duke now; she's lived that down, and I'm glad of it. Who'd thought, when Tom brought her home, that things would turn out as they have? I shouldn't know the old place, it's so changed. I expect Tom will buy it some time, and put up a grand house. Then old Patsy'll be making tracks for a new home."

Mrs. Quinn was in a talkative mood; and Mrs. Magee, who seldom interrupted her, listened smiling.

"Now, Patsy, what makes you talk like that?" she asked, after a moment's silence on the part of her companion. "You know Tom won't let you go away from us, and it does seem to me you ain't quite right to feel as you do. There ain't one of us but would work day and night for you. I'd divide my last crust with you, but it ain't my way to keep saying so."

"I know that, Mis Magee; but it's pretty hard for one like me to live as I do. There's Tom going to be some great man, and you are his mother. Katy's going to be a lady, and I'm only old Patsy Quinn, that used to take in washing, and do any kind of drudgery, just to keep soul and body together."

"Aunt Patsy, I am astonished at you!" exclaimed Katy, coming into the room in time to hear these last remarks. "I thought this kind of talk was done with." And the loving girl threw her arms about her friend's neck, and kissed the wrinkled cheek.

"I suppose it ought to be, child," was the reply. "But it seems sometimes as though my heart would break when I think of my boy. I dream about him 'most every night; and sometimes I hear him call me.

I do believe he's alive somewhere in the world."

Religion had done much for this poor woman, but it had not taken all the bitterness from her life. As she grew older, her mind naturally reverted to the past. Moreover, she anticipated the time when the young people who were now so much to her would form new ties and assume new responsibilities. Her health was less firm than it had been, and, consequently, burdens pressed more heavily.

"I guess we all need a vacation," said Tom Magee, that evening, after his mother had reported Patsy's talk. "I've been thinking about it; and, now Katy is out of school, we might go down to the sea-shore, and pitch our tent upon the sands. Wilbur Richards and I have talked over the plan, and Mrs. Richards has consented to be of the party. When Wil and I were there, last year, we wondered we had been so stupid as to leave our families at home.

There haven't been many vacations in your life, mother."

"No, my boy, not unless it's all vacation. Now, I ain't quite sure who I am, sometimes, when I put on the fine things you bring me, and look round the house. I never dreamed of having such things."

"No matter for that, mother, I've dreamed enough for a whole family; and, if all my dreams are fulfilled, I shall be the happiest man in the world."

For a moment, Mrs. Magee seemed looking through the eyes of her son. She saw a fair young girl, with starry eyes and rosebud lips; golden-brown hair, rippling over a pure, white brow, and bound in heavy tresses around a shapely head; a graceful figure, outlined against a bit of blue sky. Only a moment she saw this. Presently, there were two figures, and the bit of blue sky glowed in the fading sunlight.

Patsy Quinn, to whom the two words "vacation" and "recreation" failed to suggest their true import, could hardly be persuaded to join the party of pleasure-seekers. She wished to remain at home and look after the garden. Indeed, she made so many objections that her friends were sorely tried. Tom Magee, however, persevered in his intentions, and, at last, had the satisfaction of seeing her as much interested as he could desire.

Her childhood's home had been by the sea. She surprised Tom by telling him this the night before they were to leave home. "It was further down the coast than we are going," she said. "I could manage a boat as well as my brothers when I was a girl; but I haven't seen the ocean since I was twenty years old. I used to imagine it talked. I wonder what it would say to me now. It's like going back, my lad; though likely you'll think me a foolish old woman. I never'll be the same again after I've heard the waves roar, and seen the tide come in. But I want to go; I couldn't stay away now. Tom, do you think my boy's alive?"

"I don't think," was the reply. "I've no means of judging. Have you, Patsy?"

"No, my lad, only the feeling," she answered. "Good-night."

In many ways Patsy Quinn was more to Tom Magee than his mother could be. One had influenced him, counselled him, and exercised a sort of authority over him. The other had loved him, and trusted him in all things. One would not hesitate to reprove him if she thought him in the wrong; the other could not be made to believe that he would do wrong.

Once, when occasion seemed to demand, Patsy had said to the young man sharply, "Don't be foolish with Kate. Treat her as you would a sister. Wait till she's grown up before you try to make her think any more of you than she does now. She's a right to have her own mind."

"So she has," the young man had answered frankly. "Thank you for reminding me of my duty. It is well for me that

I have a friend at my elbow to tell me of my faults."

"Don't bear me ill-will, my lad," she responded in a tone sufficiently gentle. "You know I love you both."

"I know you do, Patsy. I bear you no ill-will. We are good comrades, as we have been since you gave me shelter one dark night."

He remembered all these things as he sat alone after she had left him. She had given him a new proof of her confidence by entrusting him with the secret she had carefully guarded for years, and he resolved that she should never want home or friend while he lived.

It was a glorious morning when they pitched their tents in the shadow of a great rock, and made preparations for housekeeping in primitive style. Everybody assisted in doing this, and everybody was in jubilant spirits. Mrs. Richards had come to please her son, but before night she was as enthusiastic in her praises of their accommodations as was Katy Moran. They were perfectly comfortable, and determined to enjoy to the full every moment of their vacation.

Fish was to be had for the catching, and Patsy, who had not forgotten her skill in preparing it for the table, installed herself as mistress of the one iron kettle which was expected to do duty in such various capacities. She could broil fish on the coals to a nicety that would tempt an epicure. She could bake fish in an oven of her own construction, and so vary their bill of fare that no one tired of the staple article.

"She seems to the manner born," said Wilbur Richards, after some grand display of her ability. "To tell the truth, Tom, the more I see that woman, the more of a mystery she is to me. Do you know that she spends most of her leisure time looking off on the sea, as though she was expecting her ship to come sailing in?"

"I *do* know it," was the reply. "Patsy's life has been a tragedy; and yet she seldom betrays the fact."

"How long have you known her?"

"Since I was ten years old. She has lived at Lion's Mouth since then, and there has never been a time when I didn't heartily like her. That woman is one of my dearest friends, and she shall never want while I have hands to work."

"And do you know anything of her son?"

"Only what she has told me, and that is but little. I fancy he was like his mother in disposition and ability. If living, he is forty years of age, and a besotted drunkard, unless he has reformed. I know enough of him to feel sure of that."

Just then Mrs. Quinn came across the sands. She was going to her accustomed place of resort, from which she saw white-sailed vessels in the distance, and noted the varying scenery of the clouds.

What said the sea to her as it sighed and moaned, and murmured? What said the waves as they came nearer and nearer, foam-crested, gleaming, silver white in the sunlight. Was it the requiem for dead hopes which she heard, or the prophecy of a glad future? Whichever it was, she was strangely moved, strangely fascinated; just for the hour, she was a child again.

A strand of gray hair, swept across her face, broke the spell which had bound her. In the bitter agony of that return to actual life, she had need to remember that "the Lord reigneth," and that "not a sparrow falleth to the ground without our Heavenly Father's notice."

Katy Moran went in search of her; but, seeing her so absorbed, turned away without speaking. Mrs. Magee saw nothing in her friend's conduct to excite curiosity; but to the other members of the party she was an object of peculiar interest. She did not care to sit or walk with them. She gathered shells merely to throw them back to the waves which had brought them to her feet. Yet she was not unsocial or gloomy as she officiated in the capacity of cook. Here she was perfectly at home, refusing all assistance, and laughingly claiming her just meed of praise.

Mrs. Richards watched her closely. Between these two there had never been a cordial expression of personal sympathy. Mrs. Quinn, keenly sensitive to the difference in their social position, was not easily won to frankness. At first, also, Mrs. Richards had failed to see the real strength of a character which lacked the refining influences of culture and education. A common interest had drawn them together; but never did the poor woman forget that her Christian sister was richly dowered with this world's goods.

"I am afraid I shall never win your friend's confidence," said Mrs. Richards to Tom Magee. "I seem to be further from it than I was the first day we met. Then I suppose there was but little to win. Under some circumstances, Mrs. Quinn would have been a magnificent woman. I have a great admiration for her."

"I am glad that you have," was responded heartily. "Patsy—I can't learn to call her by any other name—is a constant stimulus to me, and yet I have never pitied any human being as I pity her. I can't quite express my feelings for her. If ever woman was robbed of her birthright, she has been; and, if ever woman drained the cup of bitterness to its very dregs, Patsy Quinn is that woman. Her husband was a brute like many others, no worse, but her capacity for loving and suffering made every sorrow doubly keen. She is as true a friend as one can find, the wide world over. She stood by me when no man could have done for me what she did."

"But do you never think that you are growing away from her, my friend?"

"No, Mrs. Richards," answered the young man. "I may have more knowledge of the world and of books, but she has the strong common sense and intuitive perception of what is best that supplies all other deficiencies. I wish she was rich. Then she would do herself something like justice, and show the best side of her nature. She would adapt herself to the situation more easily than you imagine, if she was under no obligation to others."

Mrs. Richards bowed an assent to this, and resolved in some way to come nearer to this woman who could call forth such enthusiastic praise. Even Katy Moran was troubled in regard to Aunty Patsy, who talked so much less than usual; and the young girl ventured to ask the reason of this.

"It's because I have so much thinking to do," was the response. "Don't mind me, but just go on your own way, and, when we get back home, I'll make up the talking."

"But just tell me one thing, Aunt Patsy. Are you having a good time?"

"Yes, child, yes. I wouldn't missed coming here for anything. I mean to come every year."

"And may I come with you?"

"Yes, child. Now go to your pleasuring, and I'll look out for the old woman."

The vacation was all which had been anticipated. Many pleasant acquaintances were formed, many pleasant memories treasured. No one of the party would be quite the same after this experience. A new impulse had been given to their lives. They had breathed a pure atmosphere, and, looking out upon the broad expanse of waters they had felt their souls quickened and elevated.

"And what said the sea to you?" asked Tom Magee of Patsy Quinn.

"It said, 'Wait, Wait!' That is what it said, my lad, and I am going to wait the Lord's will and the Lord's time. He's took care of me so far, and I'm going to trust him for the rest. He knows what's best, and he knows what's going to happen, so I needn't worry about it. I don't suppose he's ever disappointed. Do you, Tom?"

"Not as we count disappointment," was the reply. "But it seems to me that sometimes he expects better things of Christians than they give."

"It's a great thing to be a *good* Christian, Tom."

"Yes, the greatest and the grandest. To do all things for the glory of God, rather than for one's own emolument, and so order our lives that others will take knowledge of us that we have been with Jesus. This is the Christian's duty."

"Yes, my lad, that's the way I think, though I never could said it. But I can say one thing. There's a good many Christians don't live as they ought to. Ministers, too, drinking wine, and making excuses for it by telling about the miracle when

Christ turned water into wine. I don't know but that was such wine as they drink in Captain Blood's saloon, but I don't believe it; and if it was, I don't believe the Saviour would make such wine now."

"I agree with you," said the young man earnestly. "Whenever I hear of a minister who finds it necessary to refer often to Christ's miracle in Cana of Galilee, I think he needs a new baptism of the Holy Spirit. If every professing Christian would heartily and consistently oppose liquor selling and liquor drinking, the temperance millennium would not be long delayed. Compromising with this terrible evil, and making apologies for it, by those who have promised to live in all things as becometh the children of God, is one of the crying sins of the church."

Not at home only did Tom Magee express this opinion. He lost no opportunity for repeating it, urging upon Christians, their duty, and stimulating them to earnest work in behalf of suffering humanity. Wilbur Richards was with him, heart and hand, their friendship so strong, and their sympathy so entire, as to provoke much good-natured criticism. Either would count, too, in whatever cause he could be enlisted.

A month had elapsed, after the return from the sea, when a visitor appeared at Lion's Mouth. The family were seated around the supper-table, plenty within and without. Life was so beautiful, home so dear, and hearts so glad. Bread had not been broken, when the door-bell was rung violently.

"I will answer that ring," said Patsy Quinn, rising.

At the door stood a tall, sunburnt man, who looked at her for a moment before saying, "I was told that Mrs. Quinn lived here."

"Yes, I am Mrs. Quinn," the woman made answer.

"Mrs. Patsy Quinn?"

"Yes."

"Then you are my mother."

No wonder that the mother fell senseless to the floor. Tom Magee was by her instantly, and, pushing aside the stranger, raised her in his arms.

"I am Holton Quinn. She is my mother," was the explanation given by the new-comer. "It can't be she's dead?"

"I think not," was the reply. And even then, through the speaker's mind flashed the thought that it might be necessary for him to protect his friend against this man who called himself her son.

Kate Moran, who was first to think of the courtesy due to Holton Quinn, asked him to enter the house.

"Thank you," he replied, in a choked voice. "I didn't mean to tell her sudden, but I couldn't help it." Refusing the chair set for him, he stood, watching the efforts made for the relief of his mother. Occasionally, a long-drawn sigh escaped him; but, aside from this, only his heavy, labored breathing betrayed emotion. At length her breast heaved, and she gasped convulsively. "Thank God!" then ejaculated the man fervently, as the hot tears rained down his cheeks.

His mother glanced around in a strange, bewildered way, looking from one to another, as though seeking some explanation. Her lips moved before she could clothe her thoughts in words.

Meanwhile, Tom Magee scrutinized the face of the stranger, seeking for some resemblance to her he claimed as mother.

"I dreamed my boy had come," whispered Patsy Quinn. "Was it a dream, or—"

"Mother! mother!" cried the sunburnt man, kneeling beside the couch on which she rested, "I am your boy Holton, come back to live with you. I've been wicked and cruel and reckless. But I'm trying to do better. Will you help me, mother? You didn't quite forget your boy, did you, mother?"

They were alone. The scene was too sacred for intrusion. In an adjoining room, there were three who wept tears of sympathy as they listened to the murmuring voices of mother and son. They did not heed the flight of time. It might have been half an hour, or it might have been much longer, when a door opened, and Patsy called, "Come here, Tom. I want you and your mother, and Katy. This is my boy," she said, as they came at her request. "I know he is; and, Holton, this is Tom Magee, and this is his mother, and this is our Katy." In token of friendship, each gave a hand to the stranger. "And, Tom, my boy's a Christian," continued Patsy. "He says he is, and he wouldn't tell me what isn't true. I want somebody to thank God for his coming back to me. I want you to pray right here."

Words of prayer came naturally to the lips of Tom Magee, and now from a full heart did he offer praise and thanksgiving.

"Amen," responded Holton Quinn earnestly. And, when they rose from their knees, he grasped the hand of his new-found friend, and, looking into the clear, honest eyes, exclaimed: "You're just the man I wanted to find."

Patsy Quinn was so happy, so glad, as she herself expressed it, that she quite forgot the untasted supper. "My wants are all supplied now," she said, laughing. Then, a moment after, turning to her son, and pushing back the hair from his forehead, she remarked, "I remember just how you looked when you bid me good-by. I never thought but you'd come back that night, and now it's been twenty-four years. We've lived a good while since then, my boy."

"Yes, mother."

To be called "mother" once more was enough to repay her for all she had suffered. Her face was transfigured with the happiness which had come to her.

How long she would have remained oblivious to all physical wants, I cannot say. Mrs. Magee, however, recovered sufficiently from her surprise to be mindful of her duties as a hostess. Mrs. Quinn must for the time be considered a guest. The supper-table was rearranged, and the happy family gathered around it.

"I don't want a mouthful to eat," said Patsy. "You'll have to put up with my ways the best you can, till I get a little used to my boy. I should been 'most afraid of him, if he hadn't told me he was a Christian. He hain't told me much else but that."

"No, mother, I haven't had time," responded her son, smiling. "But I've a long story to tell you when you're ready to hear it. California miners are great story-tellers."

"And have you been a California miner?" asked Tom Magee.

"Yes; I went out among the first. I've roughed it a good many years. I've led a hard, wild life; and I shouldn't come back now, if it hadn't been for the hope of seeing my mother, and keeping a promise made to an old comrade who died two years ago. He left a mother behind him when he went out, and I promised to find her if she was living."

"And did you?" asked Mrs. Quinn.

She has been dead five years; but I found her son and a daughter living in the old home down in Connecticut. I have been there two weeks," added the speaker. "I brought enough with me that belonged to Bill to set them up in the world."

"How did you know where to look for me?"

"I didn't know, only I found the woman that lived next door to us when we went off, and she told me that somebody see you over here, the other side of the river. So I come on, and begun to look round. I reckon I've asked a hundred times if anybody knew Mrs. Patsy Quinn, and never got track of you till to-night. I asked a man on the bridge, and he directed me here; but I didn't expect to find you in such a house as this."

"You thought I was a poor old woman, and lived in a poor old house," responded Mrs. Quinn, smiling through her tears. "Well, you see, here's Tom getting up in the world, and keeps hold of me, so I go up with him part way. This is *his* home and his mother's, and I stay with them."

"There are two sides to that story," Tom Magee hastened to say. "Sometime I will tell you what your mother has done for us, and how much we are indebted to her."

Did they like Holton Quinn? This was the question which constantly recurred to Katy Moran, who was silent while others talked.

But for a certain air of confident assurance, his manners would have been awkward. His face was strongly marked. Dissipation and hardship had left deep lines on the broad, high forehead and around the firm, well-closed lips. He had led a hard, wild life, as one well-versed in physiognomy would have known at a glance. Yet he had a genial smile, which quite illumined his rugged face; and, at times, the tones of his voice were soft and tender as a woman's.

He cared as little for supper as did his mother; and soon both returned to the parlor.

"Do you believe in him?"

Kate Moran eagerly proposed the question, and Tom Magee replied, "Yes, I do. Do you distrust him?"

"I don't think I distrust him," was her reply. "But I'm sure he *has* been a dreadfully wicked man."

Dreadfully wicked! This young, pure girl could not imagine such depths of degradation and infamy as those into which Holton Quinn had plunged. If his hands were not stained with the blood of his fellows, it was because an overruling Providence had restrained him when rage and hate would have made him a murderer. An iron constitution, and, for the last ten years, a life in the mountains, where every breeze gave new tone and vigor to the human system, had combined to preserve him from the physical degeneracy incident to a vicious career. He was, even now, a man whose strength and powers of endurance were wonderful.

His mother, in her joy, scarcely thought of the past, until he asked some questions in regard to his father's death. Then, seeing that she did not choose to speak much of this, he enquired how she lived.

"Alone, for years and years," was her reply. "I hated everybody; and myself worst of all. 'Twas a hard time for me, but I was wicked and rebellious, and that made it worse. It 'most killed me when you went off, though I didn't blame you for wanting to get away. If you'd only told me you was going, and let me known where you was!"

"I ought to, mother. But when I went

off that morning, I hadn't made up my mind certain; and after that—it's no use talking about. Can you forgive me for all these years, mother?"

"Why, yes, Holton. I hain't had a hard thought of you, for so long I can't remember. If *I'd* been different, you'd been. If I'd told you about God and heaven, you'd known better than you did."

"Yes, mother. But a good many boys go wrong that have been learnt all about God and heaven. I've seen them; and sometimes they're worst of all; though I've noticed that, when they get into a hard place, they remember and try to pray. That was the way with my old comrade, Bill Sanford. And I'm just as sure he was a Christian when he died, as I am that you're my mother. Bill and I mated fifteen years; and there wa'n't nothing we kept from each other. Poor Bill! 'Twas a dark day for me when he died. Don't blame yourself for anything I've done," continued Holton

Quinn. "If we've found the good way at last, we'll try and walk in it. I've got a pile big enough to give us what we want for the rest of our lives."

"You mean you've got money, Holton?"

"Yes, or what amounts to the same thing. You needn't do another day's work as long as you live. But how came you to be living with Tom, as you call him?"

"It's a long story to tell it all, but I'll make it short as I can," answered Patsy Quinn; and then she proceeded to give a sketch of her life for the last ten years. She related the circumstances of her first acquaintance with Kate Moran, and thus made her son somewhat acquainted with the individual history of each member of the family.

"You found good friends, mother; and more shame to me for leaving you as I did, when I might stayed and took care of you," was Holton Quinn's comment. "But we'll let bygones be bygones. I'll try and make up for it as well as I can; and 'twill be strange, mother, if we can't make something of life after all. I've got enough, if I never add a fip to it."

The evening advanced. Tom Magee went out and returned, yet still mother and son were engaged in close converse. At length the man rose to go. It was necessary that he should return to his hotel; but the next morning would find him early at Lion's Mouth. His mother watched him from the gate until his figure was lost in the darkness. Then she entered the house, saying, more to herself than to her friends: "It's all like a dream."

"It's all like a story," responded Kate Moran. "I'm just as glad as I can be; but that big man has spoiled one of my plans. I had a plan about you, Aunt Patsy, and I suppose that man has one too."

Holton Quinn was not quite sure of his plan, beyond a positive determination to make his mother's last days the brightest and best of all her life. Her friends he mentally adopted as his own. They should share his prosperity. He would find some way of assisting Tom Magee, who was, as he had said, just the man he wanted to find. His mother, too, was such a woman as he wanted to find; so strong, so brave, so true, that he could not but respect her. Had she weakly yielded to her fate, he would have pitied and loved her as his mother; but now, as a woman, he respected her. This to him was great gain, and, with new emotions of gratitude, he thanked God for the mercies which crowned his life.

Early the next morning, he went again to visit his mother, who welcomed him cordially and affectionately. "I like you better than I expected to," he remarked to her when they were by themselves.

"Why, Holton Quinn!" she exclaimed. "What do you mean?"

"Mean what I say," he replied, with his rare smile. "I've thought about you so much the last three or four years, and imagined you in all kinds of places, that I got so I couldn't remember how you used to looked. This morning, you begin to look natural to me; and I'm glad you're just such a woman as you be."

"I'm glad if you're suited," answered Patsy Quinn heartily. "I'm suited with my boy; so I guess we'll get along together. But what should I done if you'd come back bad?"

"I shouldn't come back bad," was the quick response. "I ain't nowhere near perfect now; but, if I wa'n't different from what I'd used to be, you never'd seen me."

"How came you to change?" now asked the mother. "I know 'twas by God's grace; but there was a way to bring it round."

"Yes, mother, and 'twas a strange way with Bill and me. We was shut up together twelve days in the mountains, half starving and ready to die, and there the

Lord found us. Bill's mother was a pious woman; and when he was a little shaver she made him learn whole chapters of the Bible, and some way he didn't forget them, so but what they all come back to him in time of need. That was a time of need, I tell you, mother. 'Most anybody can die game when there's a crowd looking on, but to be starved out like a grizzly in a hole in the rocks is a different thing. We was prospecting when a snow-storm come in, and we took to the first shelter. We was used to roughing it, and we'd look death in the face more than once without flinching, but 'twas a tough job up there. At first we didn't count it much; but before we got through we found out it meant something. It meant that we'd come to the end and got to turn round, though we didn't know it till we'd been there about eight days."

In relating this strange experience to his mother, Holton Quinn passed rapidly over it; but afterwards, when talking with Tom

Magee, he told in thrilling words how, one after another, all efforts to escape from their prison-house failed, until they cried unto God for deliverance.

Up to this time their lives had been of the lowest and vilest. They could not only outwork, but they could outdrink and outswear their companions, as they often boasted, and as no one would have presumed to deny. And yet they were not wholly bad. Either would have sacrificed his life for the other; and if a comrade sickened, they were first to minister to his wants.

At last, these two men found themselves, literally, in a cleft of the rocks; the falling snow fast obliterating every landmark, and the cold becoming more intense. Eating sparingly of such food as they carried, and wrapping their blankets about them, they lay down to sleep, reckless of danger. After unbroken slumbers of ten or twenty hours, as the time might be, they woke to find it still dark, and again composed themselves to sleep. Another waking, and they began to realize their situation.

"Snowed up!" exclaimed Bill Sanford, with an oath, and both groped their way about what was now a cavern, until their hands came in contact with the yielding snow.

"A warm blanket," remarked Holton Quinn. Seeking to learn the thickness of this blanket, he thrust in his arm, then his long, stout walking-stick. As this was withdrawn, a faint glimmer of light greeted them for a moment. They enlarged the aperture, and through this saw something of nature's working during their imprisonment. They felt also the stinging cold, and decided to remain in their present quarters. Walking over the newly fallen snow would be impossible. Meanwhile, they calculated their chances of living. Their stock of liquor was small, and their store of provisions scanty. They had often lived on short rations; but here they would soon be reduced to no rations at all, unless they could get out of that hole and run across a grizzly. Then there'd be a chance for a fight, and that was better than dying without any chance. Thus they talked, emphasizing nearly every word with an oath, taking in vain the name of that God who held their lives in his hand.

Their condition was fearful. To men less inured to hardship it would have been desperate. Yet they were not quite despairing, even when they began to suffer from the cravings of hunger. It was the sixth day of their imprisonment when they pushed their way again into the world, and, as Providence allowed, engaged in a fight with a grizzly, in which they won the game. There was no longer danger of starvation, but, so far as they could see, escape from their perils was impossible. They could not retrace the steps by which they had reached this point—were not even sure of the direction they had come.

More nearly disheartened than ever before,

and, truth to tell, more positively free from the influence of intoxicating drink than they had been for years, they returned to their cave, taking with them as much of their game as they could carry. They were little inclined to sleep. In the gathering darkness they could not see each other's faces, yet each could feel the beatings of the other's heart.

Bill Sanford was first to break the silence: "We've pulled together a good many years, Holt."

"Yes; and we'll pull together a good many more, Bill. I ain't going to die yet, nor you neither. There'll be a thaw and a freeze, and then we'll find our way back to camp. There's twenty years more wear in us."

"And after that, what?" asked Bill Sanford, half under his breath.

"I've nothing to do with it," was the reply. "'Tain't my lookout."

"Whose is it, Holt?"

"I don't know. What ails you, Bill?"

"Nothing, only I've been thinking about my mother. I dreamt about her last night. Poor mother, I've made her a good deal of trouble. I wish I hadn't."

Holton Quinn would have responded to this in his usual style, had not some impulse sealed his lips. When, soon after, he attempted a jest in regard to their situation, his companion sighed audibly. Another attempt was no more successful. "Out with it, Bill," he exclaimed. "'Tain't no use keeping back." And this assertion was followed with a terrible oath.

"Don't, Holt! Don't swear so. My mother didn't allow me to swear, and seems as though she could hear. I wish I'd done as she wanted me to all through. 'Twould been better."

The tone in which this was said awed Holton Quinn. It was the first time he had heard his companion express any regret for a life of reckless sinning. "You need some whiskey," he remarked, after some hesitation, because he knew not what to say, and the cravings of his own appetite suggested this.

"That would put the devil into me, Holt. I know that, and there's no doubt but I'd drink it for all mother."

Always mother! The long night wore away. The weather was more mild—a welcome change. The two men talked of it, congratulating themselves upon the prospect before them. In the midst of this, Bill Sanford exclaimed: "Holt Quinn, I'm the greatest sinner in the world, and you ain't much better. That's the truth. It's been coming over me ever since I dreamt about mother, and God knows I can't fight it off. Holt, did you ever hear your mother pray?"

"No," was the laconic reply.

"Then you can't know how I feel; but, as true as I'm a sinner, I believe my mother's praying for me this minute. I remember when I used to kneel down and say my prayers every night. I couldn't sleep if I hadn't. Last night they all came back to me, and I wanted to say them just as I used to."

"Then why didn't you?" was asked involuntarily.

"I was afraid of *you*, Holt." And tears stood in the eyes of Bill Sanford as he said this. For a moment his companion feared that he was going mad, and it may be that he understood this, for he hastened to add "I know what I'm talking about."

The Spirit of God was striving with this man, and before night he not only repeated aloud the prayers he had heard at his mother's knee, but he recited whole chapters from the Bible. His mother had been wise in her selection of Scripture lessons. How they impressed him now, shut up with only God and this companion, who was to him as another self!

From the first, Holton Quinn had not dared to ridicule him, and as day succeeded day another was fain to cry, "I am the greatest sinner in the world."

On the morning of the tenth day, Bill Sanford's face suddenly lightened as he exclaimed: "God has heard my prayer and forgiven my sins. O mother! I do believe your boy will be saved. And, Holt, too, I can't leave you behind," he added, seizing the hands of his friend in a firm grasp. "We've pulled together in the bad way, we must pull together in the right."

"What shall I do? Tell me?" was the response to this.

For answer were repeated what the speaker had been taught when he was a boy, and which, though forgotten for years, now came readily to his lips. At last the proud heart was humbled, the stubborn will subdued; and, although Holton Quinn felt not the ecstatic joy which thrilled his companion, he trusted in the mercy of God for salvation. For forty-eight hours, water had been trickling down the rocks, and the great snow-drifts were gradually sinking. Deliverance might be at hand. These two men knelt side by side, and prayed, pledging themselves, if their lives were spared, to live soberly and righteously, forsaking all evil habits, and striving for the best good of those about them. Then they lay down and slept peacefully until the morning dawned, clear and cold. They saw at a glance that now was the time to leave their present quarters. Breakfast prepared and eaten in true mountain style, and the blessing of God once more invoked, they set out on their perilous descent. Soon they recognized their locality, and were able to make tolerable progress, reaching the mining camp just before sunset. Here, after the exchange of greetings, which were strangely subdued, they were told that Johnny, the youngest of their number, was sick unto death.

"It's a hard place for him," said one, brushing away a tear which did honor to his manhood. "He wants somebody to pray with him, and not a man here that can do it. We're a set of heathens."

Bill Sanford stayed to hear no more. The next moment he was kneeling beside Johnny, murmuring: "God so loved the world, that he gave his only-begotten Son, that whosoever believeth on him might not perish, but have everlasting life."

"I've heard my mother read that," was whispered in reply. "I'm glad you've come back, Bill. Can't you pray? I'm going to die, and I want to go to heaven where mother is. Won't you ask God to let me. I've been wicked, but he's so good, and I'm so sorry. Ask him to forgive me. I've tried, but I don't know how, very well?"

"Let us pray," said the kneeling man reverently; and, as his voice was heard, a group of his comrades drew near to listen. "A parson couldn't done better," remarked one and another, wondering at the strange occurrence.

Later, when Bill explained this, telling them of his new experience and new resolves, they uttered no word of ridicule. The vilest recognize the necessity of some preparation for death, and death was in their midst. Moreover, many of these men had come from Christian homes, where Christian mothers had prayed and wept over erring sons.

"'Twas a different place after that," said Holton Quinn, when recounting the events connected with Johnny's death. "There wa'n't so much swearing and drinking. Bill had a meeting every Sunday; and, after a while, we got some Testaments, and the men read them a good deal. But 'twas tough work letting the drink alone—tough for Bill and me that never tried it before. It's the liquor keeps a man ugly.".

"True," answered Tom Magee. "If we could banish all intoxicating liquor from the world, there would be comparatively few crimes committed. All alcoholic drinks stimulate the passions and the natural instincts, while they deaden the moral sensibilities and benumb the brain. They transform a man into something worse than a brute."

"You're right about that," was the quick response. "Anybody that's seen as much drinking as I have knows that every time."

Holton Quinn was not certain that a settled life would suit him; but, for his mother's sake, and, it may be, for another's, he resolved to make the trial. He bought the cottage at Lion's Mouth with twice the amount of land then enclosed, and commenced the erection of a spacious house. Early in June, the new house was finished, furnished, and occupied, so far as two people could occupy so many rooms.

In the furnishing, Katy Moran's taste had been consulted; this young lady selecting every carpet, and every article intended for ornament. Everything was new, and yet everything had a cosy, home look.

"Are you satisfied?" she asked, turning to the owner of this house.

"Yes," he answered, with a smile. "*I* am satisfied, and I'm quite sure the little woman who is coming here will be. I couldn't done it myself. When you go to keeping house, Cousin Kate, I'll buy the fixin's, to pay for what you've done for me."

So these two had their secret. There was a little woman down in Connecticut who exercised a wonderful influence over the returned Californian. This woman, no longer young, and never beautiful, yet realized his ideal. She had been Bill Sanford's favorite sister; one upon whom the burdens of life had rested heavily, to be borne as only a true Christian woman can bear them.

Patsy Quinn might have divined her son's intentions, but not until told of his proposed marriage did she speak of it. Then she asked but one question: "Do you love the woman you are going to make your wife?"

"Yes, mother, as I love my own soul; and I'll make her happy," was his reply.

"Then, God bless you both!" she said, and turned away to hide her tears.

It was a quiet wedding, to which no one was invited. Only the brother and his family living in the old home witnessed the ceremony which bound together the lives of Mary Sanford and Holton Quinn. As well he might be, the husband was proud and happy to introduce his wife to the friends who welcomed her to her new home, where she was soon the centre of an admiring and loving circle.

Katy Moran, whose thoughts for the past year had been engrossed with others, now thought of herself. She wished to spend a year in some seminary, where she could pursue her favorite studies, and acquire some accomplishments in which she fancied herself deficient. There was no reason why this wish should not be gratified, and, before the winter holidays, she had won the esteem of teachers and scholars in one of the first seminaries of the country.

Here she made the acquaintance of a cousin, to whom she became strongly attached, and by whom she was persuaded to visit her mother's relatives, so that she did not return to her home until the school year had closed.

During her absence, she had changed much. Thought and feeling had matured. She was no longer a child, and, warmly as she was received, home was not the same to her that it had been. Aunt Patsy, quick to note her varying moods, saw this, and endeavored to learn the cause.

"Why, it isn't my home at all," said Katy, in answer to a direct question. "I never thought so much about it until now. Everybody else belongs here, but I don't. Mrs. Richards has some one to care for more than me, now Wilbur is married; and you, too, Aunt Patsy, I know you love me," she hastened to add. "Cousin Holton and

Cousin Mary treat me like a sister, and Aunt Ann is good as she can be. Tom says he's glad to have me here; but I've made up my mind to go back to the seminary. I can pay my expenses by teaching music, and I like that."

There was another who saw the change in this young girl, and, seeing, would not put forth his hand to detain her. "She shall have her life in her own way," said Tom Magee bravely. Even when six months had elapsed, and he knew she was forming plans which would take her from them altogether, he said the same.

To go back, however, in my story. Holton Quinn was hardly established in his new house, when he proposed to his mother's friend to enter into partnership with him for the purpose of traffic in an article whose uses were not fully understood, but which was sure to meet with a ready sale at large profits. He would furnish the entire capital, and the terms he proposed were so liberal they could not fail to be accepted. Indeed, Tom Magee was glad to engage in more active employment, and at once addressed himself to his new duties. A short trial proved that the profits of the business had not been overestimated, and, under good management, it was rapidly developed.

Of course, the junior partner, acting as book-keeper and attending to all correspondence, had little leisure; yet he still found opportunity to do much for the promotion of every good work. His old friends congratulated him upon his prospects. Jack Wetherbee, Robert Morrison, and a score of others rejoiced in his good fortune as though it had been their own.

After a time, in the prosecution of his business, it became necessary for him to visit different parts of the country; and, in a thriving Western town, he encountered Luther Marshall. A few days after this young man was forbidden to enter Captain

Blood's saloon, he had started for the West, resolved to retrieve his name and fortune, or die among strangers.

Upon a tract of land purchased by his father, he built a cabin, in which he commenced housekeeping. The very novelty of his position charmed him. He felt within him the stirrings of ambition. He was the best educated man in the township, which was being rapidly settled. He needed hard work for the development of his physical and mental strength; and of this needed discipline he had plenty. Not a drop of intoxicating liquor had passed his lips since the night Tom Magee had assisted him to his home.

At the time of their meeting, he was universally respected and trusted. His violent temper had been so controlled that he was considered a man of rare equanimity, as, indeed, he was. A good house was in process of erection, and he was soon to exchange his bachelor quarters for others more in accordance with his tastes and resources.

He *was* saved, thanks to the efforts of a faithful friend and God's blessing. He did not need to tell this friend how he had suffered and struggled. He did not care even to speak of his sufferings and struggles. He was looking forward to a future which held for him so much of happiness that the past was half forgotten. At parting, the happy man wished his friend unbounded prosperity in all things—riches and an elegant home, with a wife dear and charming as his own would be.

Within a week from that time, Tom Magee called at a young ladies' seminary, and asked to see Miss Moran. He was very impatient as he waited for her appearance; yet felt himself amply repaid when she met him with extended hands and the exclamation, "I'm *so* glad to see you!"

How her visitor replied to this she was never quite sure, although he gave abundant proof of his pleasure in seeing her. A blush had betrayed her secret; and, folded in the arms of one who loved her as few can love, she listened to the old, sweet story. "Of all the world, my darling, I would have chosen you," he murmured.

"Of all the world I would have chosen you," was the response to which he listened; and he was sure that with him Katy Moran would have her life in her own way.

All other engagements must now yield to this, which was to be lifelong; and our Katy returned to Lion's Mouth, to be welcomed as a daughter. So Mrs. Magee called her, anticipating the event which would make her a daughter in very truth.

Patsy Quinn was delighted. She always expected how things would turn out, and she took occasion to commend Tom for having taken her advice, and "let the child find out her own mind. You'll both of you be happier for it; and, if I'm any judge, you're just good enough for each other. To tell the truth, I'm so well off and so glad, that it 'most seems as though things had happened just right always. There's Holton's wife, now. She ain't like our Katy; but she is a good woman, and I think more and more of her every day I live. And as for baby, seems as though she was my very own.

There was but one who expressed any dissatisfaction with the arrangements. Holton Quinn wished the wedding to be deferred until a new house could be in readiness for the bride. He made such a proposition, claiming the right to furnish the house, and promising to have it ready for its occupants at the earliest possible moment. For once, however, the senior member of the firm found his partner obstinate. The wedding took place in the same little cottage where, as a homeless child, Katy Moran had found shelter and care.

Now that years have passed, the cottage has given place to a more pretentious dwelling; and Tom Magee holds his house and grounds by right of title-deed, and not as tenant. There are baby faces and baby voices within his home, yet never one of all so fair, so sweet to him as the face and voice of his wife.

Wilbur Richards, still his friend, knows now to what purpose were the efforts made in his behalf. But he knows not all. Not until the secrets of all hearts are revealed shall the influence of one earnest, consecrated life be fully known.

Neither can the influence of an evil life be justly estimated until the last great day. Reaching on and on through coming generations, the curse may fall upon children's children. Such men as Captain Blood of our story — they who claim the right to do as seemeth to them best, without regard to that higher law which holds all to strict account— have need to pray that upon themselves only may rest the judgment of God.

The honorable liquor-seller amassed a fortune which his boys are fast squandering;

and to-day he knows, by bitter experience, how other parents have suffered as their sons tarried long at the wine. In desperation, he sold his saloon, liquors, fixtures, and profitable trade, hoping thus to arrest the downward career of those he loved. But the honorable purchaser was no respecter of persons; and, despite the father's entreaties, sold to one as to another.

His sin has found him out, and his victims will be avenged. Peace and happiness are not to be purchased with the price of blood.

For Sunday=School Libraries.

The National Temperance Society have now published thirty-five volumes specially adapted to Sunday-School Libraries, written by some of the best authors in the world. These have been carefully examined and unanimously approved by the Publication Committee of the Society, representing the various religious denominations and Temperance organizations of the country, which consists of the following members:

Peter Carter,   T. A. Brouwer,   Rev. Alfred Taylor,
A. A. Robbins,   Rev. J. B. Dunn,   Rev. C. D. Foss,
Rev. M. C. Sutphen,   Rev. A. G. Lawson,   James Black,
J. N. Stearns,   Rev. G. L. Taylor,   R. R. Sinclair,
            Rev. William Howell Taylor.

TO SUNDAY-SCHOOL SUPERINTENDENTS AND TEACHERS:

You will probably agree with us that the main hope of saving the community from the terrible evils and the widening curse of Intemperance lies in *saving the young*. If the hearts and the habits of the children are not established in Christian sobriety, the next generation will be worse than the present. This work of enlightening and instructing the children on this great question of health, happiness, and vital religion, devolves largely upon the Sabbath-School.

And it is exceedingly important that the Teachers should add to their own personal instructions the circulation of excellent books among their classes. Every Sabbath-School Library should contain a well-selected collection of books, to set forth the dangers of the Intoxicating Cup, and the duty and safety of early abstinence.

The National Temperance Society and Publication House, under the presidency of Hon. William E. Dodge, and the management of leading men of all denominations, has issued a series of volumes for the young, which we cordially commend to you.

A Catalogue is herewith enclosed, with the prices attached. Will you not endeavor to introduce these excellent volumes at once into your Sabbath-School?

With fraternal wishes for the spiritual success and growth of your *training schools for Christ*.

We remain, yours in Gospel love,

STEPHEN H. TYNG, New York.   T. L. CUYLER, Brooklyn.
JOSEPH CUMMINGS, Connecticut.   H. W. BEECHER, Brooklyn.
J. B. DUNN, Boston.   JOHN HALL, New York.
C. D. FOSS, New York.   W. H. H. MURRAY, Boston.
GILBERT HAVEN, Boston.   H. C. FISH, Newark.
E. S. JANES, New York.   J. D. FULTON, Boston.

Address your orders to

J. N. STEARNS, Publishing Agent,

58 Reade Street, New York.

Temperance Sermons.

The National Temperance Society are publishing a series of Sermons upon various phases of the temperance question, by some of the leading Clergymen in America. The following are already published:

Common Sense for Young Men. By Rev. HENRY WARD
BEECHER... $0 75
Moral Duty of Total Abstinence. Rev. T. L. CUYLER 75
The Evil Beast. By Rev. T. DE WITT TALMAGE... 75
The Good Samaritan. By Rev. J. B. DUNN... 75
Self-Denial: A Duty and a Pleasure. By Rev. J. P. NEWMAN, D.D., Chaplain of United States Senate... 75
The Church and Temperance. By JOHN W. MEARS, D.D.; Professor at Hamilton College, New York... 75
Active Pity of a Queen. By Rev. JOHN HALL, D.D... 75
Temperance and the Pulpit. By Rev. C. D. FOSS, D.D. 75
The Evils of Intemperance. By Rev. J. ROMEYN BERRY, 75
Other Sermons will soon follow.

The National Temperance Advocate.

The National Temperance Society and Publication House publish a new Monthly Temperance Paper, the object of which is to promote the interests of the cause of Temperance, by disseminating light from every quarter upon its moral, social, financial, and scientific bearings. The best talent in the land will be secured for its editors and contributors. Terms—in advance: Single copy, one year, $1; 10 copies to one address, $9; 20 copies to one address, $16; all over 20 copies, at 80 cents per copy.

Band of Hope Supplies.

Band of Hope Manual, per dozen... $0 60
Temperance Catechism, " ... 60
Band of Hope Melodies, per hundred... 10 00
Certificates of Membership, " ... 3 00
Juvenile Temperance Pledges, " ... 3 00
Pledge and Certificate, combined (in colors), per hundred... 4 00
Juvenile Temperance Speaker... 25
The Temperance Speaker... 75
Four New Temperance Dialogues... 30
Band of Hope Badge, plain, $7 per dozen; enamelled, $1 25 per dozen; silver and enamelled, 50 cents each.
Illuminated Temperance Cards, sets of 10 each... 35
Illustrated Juvenile Tracts, per thousand... 3 00

The Youth's Temperance Banner.

The National Temperance Society and Publication House publish a beautifully Illustrated Monthly Paper, especially adapted to children and youth, Sunday-school and Juvenile Temperance Organizations. Each number contains several choice engravings, a piece of music, and a great variety of articles from the pens of the best writers for children in America. It should be placed in the hands of every child in the land. Terms—in advance:

Single Copies, one year. $0 25 | 30 Copies, to one address, $3 75
8 Copies, to one address, 1 00 | 40   "   "   "   5 00
10   "   "   "   1 25 | 50   "   "   "   6 25
15   "   "   "   1 88 | 100 "   "   "   12 00
20   "   "   "   2 50 |

Address J. N. STEARNS, Publishing Agent,
58 Reade Street, New York.

www.ingramcontent.com/pod-product-compliance
Lightning Source LLC
Chambersburg PA
CBHW022109290426
44112CB00008B/607